Just As I Am

Just As I Am

Journal-Keeping for Spiritual Growth

Virginia Hearn

Fleming H. Revell
A Division of Baker Book House Co
Grand Rapids, Michigan 49516

© 1994 by Virginia Hearn

Published by Fleming H. Revell
a division of Baker Book House Company
P.O. Box 6287, Grand Rapids, MI 49516-6287

Printed in the United States of America

Library of Congress Cataloging-in-Publication Data

Hearn, Virginia.
    Just as I am : journal-keeping for spiritual growth / Virginia Hearn.
        p. cm.
    Includes bibliographical references.
    ISBN 0-8007-5545-6
      1. Spiritual journals—Authorship. 2. Spiritual life—Christianity. I. Title.
    BV4501.2.H3694   1994
    248.4'6—dc20   94-31465

The phrase Intensive Journal, used in the Progoff Method, is a registered trademark.

The conversation on pages 107–9 is © Nancy Boerman.

Along with my sisters, Kathryn Long and Mildred Meythaler, five persons have particularly, profoundly influenced my life:

—Virgil Petter Blumer ("Miss Petter"), my high school Latin teacher in Monroe, Wisconsin
—Joyce Achemire Hall, who led a small dorm Bible study at Otterbein College in Ohio
—the late Joseph Bayly, then editor of InterVarsity's student magazine (HIS), and my first editorial mentor
—my always encouraging friend, Frances Adeney, now a professor at Satya Wacama Christian University in Indonesia
—my husband, Walter Hearn, who has been in dozens of my journal-keeping workshops at New College Berkeley and elsewhere, always an enthusiastic participant

This book is dedicated to them.

Contents

Acknowledgments

"There is no creation without tradition," commented Mexican writer Carlos Fuentes in his essay, "How I Started to Write." "The 'new' is an inflection on a preceding form; novelty is always a variation on the past."[1]

As I have thought about writing this book and still more as I have worked on it, I recognize my indebtedness to many other persons. I think first of Margaret Hannay and Shirley Nelson, who in 1980 led two workshops on journal-keeping at a conference of the Evangelical Women's Caucus in Saratoga Springs, New York. The hours I spent listening to their description and counsel, taking copious notes on what they said, were the primary catalyst to the direction my life has taken these past fourteen years.

Home again in California, and acting on their recommendation, I began attending every journal-keeping workshop I could find. Over the next three years I participated in at least twelve, some on journal-keeping in general, some with a particular emphasis; workshops sponsored by various organizations—academic, religious, medical, therapeutic—led by facilitators with varying outlooks and methods. Through them I gained further insights and learned new approaches to meaningful "journaling." This book now reflects some of those ideas, as I gradually discovered how to make them most relevant to my own classes at New College Berkeley. (My husband and I have served both on the board and as adjunct faculty members for this small and ever-struggling Christian study center since its founding by David Gill and others in the mid-'70s.)

I list other books on journaling in a bibliography at the end of this book. The creativity of these writers, too, has provided ideas for self-discovery and spiritual growth that have benefited me, my husband, and our daughter, Christine Hearn-Bennett. Thus, as Carlos Fuentes observed about his own writing, *Just As I Am* is an outgrowth of a many-faceted journal-keeping "tradition," both contemporary and ancient.

Equally significant has been the enthusiastic affirmation of men and women who have attended my workshops at New College and elsewhere since 1983. I am grateful to those who have allowed me to quote from their writings in this book, which now appears after a very long gestation. Intrinsic to its appearance was the gift of a newer KayPro computer from New College board member Fred Vann, after my dinosaur KayPro departed this life. Having just begun this book, I knew I could not also learn a new word-processing system at the same time.

Finally, how does any author adequately acknowledge the contribution of her behind-the-scenes publishing house editor? Bill Petersen of Fleming Revell gets five stars.

Introduction

Henry David Thoreau kept a journal. So did George Washington and John Adams. The diaries of famous Christians from the past continue to be republished and to intrigue us, like those of Jonathan Edwards, Samuel Johnson, David Brainerd, John Wesley, and Søren Kierkegaard. (John Wesley used a secret code, which has now been deciphered, in some of his journals.) Because for centuries the lives of women were given little space in history books, encyclopedias, and other biographical sources, not much could be known about their lives—were it not for the discovery and in some cases the publication of their long-overlooked diaries and journals. In recent decades the diaries of Anaïs Nin (extending over forty years), Dag Hammarskjöld, Anne Frank, Thomas Merton, May Sarton, and Henri Nouwen have been best-sellers.

Now, especially since the 1960s, a lot of ordinary men and women have begun "journaling." Anyone, of whatever age, can keep a journal—and the majority of those who make that effort describe it as surprisingly helpful. Through that practice they find new understanding, along with new meaning and direction for their lives. Certainly it is a better way to record ideas than jotting them down on the back of an envelope or on whatever scrap of paper is handy. Journal-keeping, as it is being done today, is not the same as writing in a diary as an adolescent.

A personal journal can be a remarkable aid to spiritual growth. In the Bible, God's people were frequently told to remember what the Lord had done for them. "Remember that you were a slave in Egypt, and the Lord your God redeemed you from there" (Deut. 24:18 NASB). Writing is an aid to memory. As we write, God can speak to us through our memories.

As people of faith, we want to discern God's will. We want his guidance in making big and small decisions. Sometimes we hope that writing things down will help us sort through what is going on in our lives. At such times it makes sense to take pen and paper in hand, since our thoughts often go further in writing than they would have if we just sat and analyzed (or worried about) our circumstances. When we keep a journal we are taking something that is inside us and putting it outside us, where we can look at it, ponder it, and pray about it.[1]

Later on, when we reread what we have written, we may be astonished to find "diamonds in the dust."[2] No one's life is so prosaic or uninteresting that it is not worth documenting. No one's life is unimportant to God.

> Why write? Why keep a journal?
> Though for no other cause, yet for this,
> That posterity may know we have
> Not loosely through silence
> Permitted things to pass away as in a dream.
>
> Richard Hooker[3]

Getting Started

Here goes, then. This is a painful and almost insuperable step for me: yielding up so much that has been suppressed to a blank sheet of lined paper. The thoughts in my head are sometimes so clear and so sharp and my feelings so deep, but writing about them comes hard. The main difficulty, I think, is a sense of shame. So many inhibitions, so much fear of letting go, of allowing things to pour out of me, and yet that is what I must do if I am ever to give my life a reasonable and satisfactory purpose.

Etty Hillesum
An Interrupted Life:
The Diaries 1941–43

Who needs it? I'll ask myself; but I'll write anyway. I've been grateful for uneventful days, because I've found I can be just as tired at the end of them as at the end of busy ones, but at least there's less to write. Still, it's often on days when I thought nothing happened that I'll start writing and go on for pages, a single sound or sight recalled from the afternoon suddenly loosing a chain of thoughts. I've learned, in fact, that NOTHING NEVER HAPPENS.

Thomas Mallon
A Book of One's Own

Part 1

Me? Keep a Journal? 1

Famous people sometimes keep journals, and because of their fame, other people are interested in reading what they write. Just before retiring from the army in 1993, Gen. Colin Powell, the first black man to head the U.S. Joint Chiefs of Staff, signed a six-million-dollar book contract to write his "memoirs." I don't know if this well-known and popular general kept any kind of personal journal during his years in the military, as he rose in the ranks, but I have no doubt that his memoirs would make better reading if he had.

Other people have become famous only *because* they once kept a journal; it is their journal, or diary, that has set them apart and is the source of their fame. Thirteen-year-old Anne Frank, hiding from the Nazis as they overran Holland and tracked down Jews, comes immediately to mind. With the rise of Hitler, Anne's family had emigrated to Holland from Germany in the early '30s, so Anne's diary was first written in Dutch. Within ten years of its 1947 publication in Amsterdam, it had already been translated and republished in twenty countries.

Not until 1981 did the diaries of Etty Hillesum come to light. She was a young woman in her mid-twenties, also Jewish, also living in Amsterdam during that terrifying era. Both Etty and Anne died in Nazi concentration camps—Etty at Auschwitz, Anne at Bergen-Belsen. It is their journals that survived.

But most of us are not famous for any reason, nor are we ever likely to be. Right now, as you are reading or browsing through this book, you may be thinking, "Who, me? Keep a journal? No way. Forget it." On the other hand, after a little reflection, you might be willing to admit, "Well, maybe I should have been keeping a journal when . . ." Or "I sometimes wish I'd started doing that long ago; it'd really be something to read it now."

"Journal-writing helps me see the beauty of my place in God's plan."

The person you once were—as a younger adult, teenager, or child—is now largely lost. There may have been certain periods in your life that you realize were important to your becoming the person you are today. It may have been when you first joined the Boy or Girl Scouts, your "escape" from parental overprotection. Or your discovery that you could do well in school if you just put your mind to it. Perhaps it was when you made the team or were quarterback your senior year—and nothing since has quite equaled that. Even thinking back to the time when a boy or girl you'd admired from afar finally began to notice you, you may still feel a tinge of the exhilaration of puppy love, or of real love, which was then all-consuming. Perhaps particular teachers, or some other adult, went out of their way to encourage and help you.

Some of you can date the year, even the hour, when you first understood the gospel, and you point to that as a turning point in your life. You turned *from* something *to* Someone, to the sovereign God and to Jesus his Son, and it made a significant difference in your high school, college, or adult experience.

Now, as you grow older and mature in faith, you may ponder your past: the choices you made about which school to attend, what to major in (did your choices make sense?), and what kind of friends you chose to spend time with (did they contribute to your spiritual growth? what has happened to them since graduation? what are they doing with their lives now?). There was the thrill of getting your first real job, and then perhaps a second or third; a trip to Europe with family or a friend; the decision to move to another part of the country; years of singleness and the questions raised by being "alone"; perhaps courtship, marriage, the birth or adoption of children.

So many details of those life-transforming experiences have faded and are lost. But they would not be lost if you had been keeping a journal, which you now could occasionally reread.

On the other hand, there are plenty of things you might not want to remember. Obviously not all the important events of anyone's life are positive. Yet the negative or sad ones may be influencing you, perhaps unconsciously, still today.

You may have lost your father or mother, or a sister or brother, through death. Your parents may have had angry battles right in front of your eyes and eventually divorced. Or there may have been no battles at all, but suddenly you were told that Dad was moving out; your family as you knew it had ended. Did someone whose friendship or respect you needed put you down or embarrass you in a cruel manner? Perhaps you underwent a long illness, with dull, slow hours that could have passed more quickly, more meaningfully, if you had been absorbed in keeping your very own journal.

Increasingly many women, and some men, are trying hard as adults to deal with painful memories, often long repressed, of physical or sexual abuse. Most of us have probably had one or more experiences of a special person, a boyfriend, girlfriend, fiancé(e), or spouse, choosing to walk out of our life— or simply disappearing with no explanation at all. As parents, some of us have tried for years to cope with a rebellious son or daughter, now grown into adulthood and seemingly out of the family circle forever. How does one live with the anguish of abandonments?

Even experiences like those, however, can be better dealt with when written down in your own words. That is why so many counselors and therapists ask their clients to keep a journal and bring it to their counseling sessions. One counselor writes:

> I never enter into a counseling relationship unless the person who wants my help will agree to keep a journal. This diarying stimulates spiritual growth like no other tool I know. It becomes a format by which I can direct my counselees to the One who can best help them, and that is God, the wisest Counselor.[1]

Yes, the thought of keeping a journal "someday" does recur from time to time to a lot of people. But "If not now, when?" the Jewish sage Hillel is quoted as saying. In bookstores and stationery stores, you walk by display racks of expensive, fabric-covered "blank books." You may buy one, attracted by the picture or beautiful design on its cover, even if the empty pages inside are a bit intimidating. Or a friend or relative may give you one (the perfect gift for a person who has everything). And there it is. Your journal.

If Not Now, When?

Many people decide to start keeping a journal at a time of transition in their lives. Perhaps that is true of you now. It may be that you are moving away from a former role, going against the expectations of family members or friends. Perhaps you are thinking about changing jobs, making a major career move, relocating to find work, starting off in an entirely different direction, or retiring. It may be that you are wondering about marrying someone, or have just begun a new life in a distant place with a husband or wife. This may be a time of questioning, doubt, and searching, a time of joy or sadness. Anne, a friend of mine who has been keeping a journal since she was eleven years old, decided to begin a second journal especially for her newborn daughter Roz.

Over the years a lot of Christians have kept lists of people they are praying for, along with special "prayer requests." As time goes on, if they record what has happened in those instances, that list becomes a form of journal-keeping. Some Christians experiment with writing out or typing their prayers in their personal devotional life or daily meditation time. Others may start recording chapter and verse and how a particular passage of the Bible has spoken to them. They may copy out quotations that, remarkably, seem to fit their own situation.

All kinds of people find it helpful to write down what they are going through and thinking about during periods of worry or stress, times when they are feeling especially buffeted by life. When they do, they may realize that gradually their anxiety is being alleviated through their writing. Just to see the details of a present quandary written down in black-and-white becomes a means of clarification—a first step in being able to pray realistically about the situation, get a handle on it, and make practical decisions for real-life action. Specificity in journal-writing is a help in moving beyond endless "stewing" or unconscious brooding about one's problems.

> Nine years ago, I left a job when the boss called me "worthless." I myself wondered if it were true. In the maelstrom of feelings that come up with job loss, I felt it would be useful to explore those feelings. But how? I couldn't afford a counselor. My friends were supportive, but I wanted to go really deep, and I needed confidentiality. I started a personal journal.[2]

Journal-Keeping Workshops

In 1983 I started leading journal-keeping workshops at a small graduate school, New College for Advanced Christian Studies, Berkeley (NCB), where I am still a faculty member. Since people often ask me about how I began leading such workshops I will tell that story in chapter 11. At the end of my workshops, participants hand in evaluation forms, making comments like the ones you see printed in the margins of this book.

You probably will not be making a trip to California to attend one of the New College workshops, though you might be able to find a journal workshop held near where you live, even outside the U.S.[3] Your experience in any workshop will depend on the outlook, methods, warmth, and spirit of the leader—sometimes called a facilitator—along with your own openness and willingness to participate. My husband and I led one journal workshop for couples at a Christian retreat center where several middle-aged men sat with their arms folded and glared at us for the entire weekend. Evidently they did not realize that their wives had signed them up for something other than a typical "Bible teaching" conference. Afterward, as we drove back home, we wondered what conversations took place in their cars and inside their houses over the next week or so.

What You Need to Begin

Books on the "how to" of journal-keeping abound. I try to buy such books whenever I find one, and now my own library has over fifty such guides. I always take them in two apple boxes to my workshops, so participants can see the many helps that are available. Most of these books are still in print, but some have to be special-ordered from bookstores. Many books in my collection relate directly to this topic. Others—for example, books on writing memoirs—have indirect tie-ins. (See the bibliography.)

My book collection shows the different approaches that authors take to journal-keeping, approaches usually based on what has worked best for them. I learn from their suggestions, picking up new ideas to use for myself and to try out in my workshops.

After years of keeping a journal, some of these writers now find themselves with shelves of the blank books I referred to above—though theirs are no longer blank. Others suggest that prospective "journalers" avoid buying those brightly colored, artfully designed, bound volumes. Blank books do have the advantage of fitting into a large purse or briefcase, so you can carry them around wherever you go and write in them at will, but their bound-in pages will limit you to a strictly chronological approach in journal-keeping. And woe to the person who decides to eliminate or shift any of those pages around to another place. Another major disadvantage of blank books is that before long it becomes hard to find paragraphs or ideas you're sure you've written about previously. You know they are there somewhere. But where?

I think it is more practical to buy an ordinary three-ring loose-leaf notebook for journal-keeping.[4] First of all, loose-leaf notebooks are inexpensive, and, if you watch for back-to-school sales, even in the inflationary '90s you can find three-ring notebook paper for a penny a sheet, sometimes less. You need not lug this large notebook around with you (it's safer not to—you might lose it), but you can easily carry a small sheaf of three-ring paper for the odd times when you may have a chance to write.

Then, as your journal-keeping continues, and the pages in your notebook reach into the dozens, and hundreds, you can easily devise a number of categories or divisions to classify the different aspects of your now-voluminous output. Further, within these categories, you can still place your writing chronologically. Finally, should it become important to do so, you can remove or relocate pages without destroying the book's visual integrity.

As we move on, I will suggest a number of journal-keeping categories, or sections, that can be separated in your notebook by inexpensive loose-leaf dividers, to help you organize your writing and thus make it more accessible to you. In time you will probably think of other, supplementary categories to fit the topics you personally find yourself writing about most often. If you are into computer lingo, this is simply a way to establish your own "file directories."

What else do you need? Well, only a pen (preferably) or pencil—and perhaps a small box of those small white-circle reinforcements to paste in when your journal gets such heavy usage that its pages start to tear out. Then, too, as you write more, you can buy additional binders in which to store your accumulating pages.

Your Own Journal Workshop

Psychotherapist Ira Progoff, the father of contemporary American journal-keeping,[5] sometimes says, "Give yourself a journal workshop." To set aside a weekend morning or afternoon (or both) to work in your journal might turn out to be the best possible use of that time. The New College workshops begin on Friday night for two hours, continue for five and a half hours on Saturday morning and afternoon, and conclude with two and a half hours on Sunday afternoon. On its descriptive flyer, participants are asked to commit themselves to the workshop for the full ten hours. On Friday night I forewarn everyone that they will probably be very tired by the end, since the entire time is spent in serious reflection and extensive writing.

Some people come in the door the first evening saying, "I don't know about this. I'm not very good at writing." I assure them that such an apprehension is common, and that, because of the mostly small segments that comprise the weekend's writing, they *will* be able to do it.

To get started, I take half an hour or so to talk about journal-keeping as distinct from writing in a daily diary. Most journal exercises during the weekend are about an assigned topic, and participants have a brief time frame for the writing, usually ten to thirty minutes. In one book on journal-keeping, the authors point out that diary entries generally tell what and when, and sometimes how and why, but a journal "is about *who*—who the writer is—who you are." That makes it a "book that only you can write."[6]

Two other experienced journal-keepers assure beginners that this kind of writing is not an antisocial or narcissistic process, as some skeptics might charge. What you write will have implications for your life and will have an effect on it. But, they counsel, it is not a substitute for prayer, meditation, Bible study, or a personal devotional life. Nor is it a substitute for therapy or professional counseling, if you need that.[7]

As you get into journal-keeping, it is important that it not become a "new legalism," something you force yourself to do every day—and then flagellate yourself mentally if you don't keep it up regularly. A lot of us vigorously maintain that we are "saved by faith" but then live as if our eternal destiny depended on what we do, on whether or not we are "good enough." As a result of such thinking, we already have a lot of legalism in our lives, and we may be prone to make journal-keeping, which *can* be an aid to spiritual growth, just one more rule to live by.

"Putting my thoughts into categories has given me hope for depth in my journaling. It has given it some needed focus."

Instead, try to think of journal-keeping as a gift you give yourself, a spiritual gift. You honor the fact that God made you and loves you by making time for yourself: time to be quiet, relax, reflect, and write. It's a way to step off the treadmill of feeling driven, to back off from what one writer describes as the "tyranny of the urgent."[8]

Your journal will become a record of the real you at a particular time and place, and as you look it over later, you will begin to understand that record. You will gain some perspective on where you've been, where you are now, and where you may be going. Journal-keeping has past-, present-, and future-tense aspects.

English essayist G. K. Chesterton wrote, "Our minds are mostly a vast uncatalogued library."[9] What would happen if there were no Dewey Decimal or Library of Congress systems for shelving library books? Imagine the chaos that would result and the virtual impossibility of ever finding anything.

Through journaling, you can become aware of whatever order already exists in your life. As you journal you can also reorder your priorities and your use of time. You can bring some unity to the complexity of your responsibilities and experience. Novelist and poet May Sarton described her journal-writing as a "thread of continuity" underlying tumultuous days. The journal is a good way to sort out events, she said. "I find it wonderful to have a receptacle into which to pour vivid momentary insights, and a way of ordering day-to-day experiences."[10]

Continuing Sarton's "thread metaphor," I have adapted an image I found in a very early pamphlet on journaling:

> Journal-keeping is like having a cardigan sweater with two pockets. The left-hand one is full of a tangle of string. In the right-hand one is a small ball of neatly wound string. When you have time, you take out the tangle and wind a piece of it onto the tidy ball. And slowly, slowly, the tangle gets smaller and the ball gets larger.[11]

In your own journal, as in a diary, you will record some memories, but it is also important to describe your reaction to whatever you are writing about. That is essential to the "untangling."

Your journal can also help you make decisions and plot the evolution of your decisions. If you write honestly, on rereading parts of it later, you will be amazed at some of the things you thought and wrote. In its pages you will discover a complex and fascinating individual.

There is also a certain mystique in just getting words down on paper. Sometimes the ideas flowing out of your pen will surprise you. You will see that the "shaping of ideas can occur on paper," and as a result you are able to talk more easily with others. "Journal-keeping unblocks words."[12] That is exactly what we shy or less verbal people need.

The subtitle of this book relates journal-keeping to potential spiritual growth. Each person, however, will bring to the writing his or her own religious outlook; this process isn't limited to Protestants, Catholics, Presbyterians, Baptists, high-church or low-church types. People of different faiths, or even of no traditional faith, have come to the New College workshops and found it a positive experience to listen to the thoughts of others who, like them, openly and honestly share spiritual concerns. For once, these persons hear the voices of sensitive, humble Christians, so different from the common media caricature of evangelicals or "born-againers."

"Self-knowledge . . . ," wrote Elizabeth O'Connor, "is essential for spirituality. . . . When we commit our observations to writing . . . we are holding a piece of our life in our hands where we can look at it, meditate on it, and deepen our understanding of it."[13] Although reading aloud is not required in the New College journal workshops, people are given opportunities to read aloud brief parts of what they have written, should they choose to do so.[14] In that way, participants are bonded in their humanness. They see that they have many experiences and problems in common. When they realize that, a wonderful spirit of empathy develops—which is surely one small step toward peace in this world.

Nothing Never Happens 2

Although we are seldom conscious of it, the world keeps turning on its axis. As long as our life on earth continues, there is always more to say, always more to write in our journals. Something is always going on, outside us and inside us. "*Nothing* never happens."

> In our journals we are in search of the real self—of what really moves us, what we really think, what we really feel. . . . The pages of a journal kept over the days and weeks and months will help us in our pursuit of truth—in making God our aim.[1]

Are you ready to begin journal-keeping? The way to begin is to begin. To build momentum, here are several guidelines I have found to be useful.

1. Always put the date at the top of every page you write. It also helps to note the place where you are writing and sometimes the time of day as well. And don't forget the year. Years later, that won't be so obvious as it is today.

2. Then stop; don't start—not yet. Wait. Put down your pen, close your eyes, and take a minute or two to be quiet, turn inward, and *listen*. Some individuals find it helpful to count slowly up to their present age. Others try to pay attention to

their breathing as it becomes slower. To do this is a way to calm down, to learn the meaning of what Quakers call "centering." Many people in my workshops have commented on the importance of first observing a few minutes of quiet, rather than immediately rushing ahead with what they think they want to write about.[2]

The Journal-writer is—	The Journal-writer is not—
• an observer	• a censor
• a reporter	• a judge
	• an analyst
	• a psychoanalyst

3. From time to time, review parts of what you have previously written. This is important in journal-keeping. But when you reread, don't go over your earlier sentences and paragraphs to change or soften what you find there. Forget the existence of erasers and white-out. Think of your journal-keeping as if you are an on-the-scene reporter rather than a zealous editor with blue pencil in hand. However . . .

4. After rereading a passage in your journal, take time to write a response to what you have just read. When you do this, if you want to change, correct, or qualify something, you can now add that at the end. (Here you see the advantage of having a notebook into which you can insert extra pages.) And be sure to date this new segment and your additional insights as well.

5. If you live with other people, keep your journal off the "beaten path." Don't tempt your housemates to pick it up and read it because it's right there in plain sight on the living-room coffee table. You might ask them, as a point of honor if necessary, *not* to read it, should they happen to come across it.

On the other hand, your journal shouldn't be hard for you to get to. If you have to go to the basement for a stepladder, climb to the top shelf of a closet, lift out your high-school saxophone from where it is stored, and then reach on tiptoe for your journal, it is clear that you will not be writing in it very often.

After awhile you may start to feel like this man, a long-time journal-keeper:

> There are about thirty of them now—notebooks of different sizes, every page of them filled up with handwriting. . . . I have in them a thousand things to cheer me up. . . . I can remember just how I felt that Friday night. . . . My own diaries have outgrown the green strongbox I used to keep them in, and I've outgrown believing I'm such a shocking character that they need to be locked up. They're a permanent part of life now. . . .[3]

Some Warm-Up Exercises

It makes sense to start off in journal-keeping by buying several packages of three-ring notebook dividers, along with the notebook itself and a supply of loose-leaf paper. I call the first divider category *Who Am I?* It will contain all kinds of short miscellaneous (or warm-up) exercises, including those that don't readily fit into any other section. That makes the *Who Am I?* category sort of a catch-all (something like that hall closet where your saxophone from high school now resides).

Begin every journal-writing exercise with a clean sheet of paper and date it. You may decide to do only one exercise each evening for the first few days. You know how your muscles feel the next day if you overdo it when you begin a new fitness regimen. So start off slowly and thoughtfully.

What Time Is It in My Life?

Record the date, perhaps in the upper left-hand corner. Then, on the first line, or in the space at the top of the page, write this question: "What Time Is It in My Life?" If you tend to be a visual person, you may want to draw a small clock off to one side and fill in the numbers. After a minute or so of relaxing, you might fill in hands on the clock to show a specific time of day. Then, write a paragraph or two in answer to this obviously metaphorical question.[4] Here are several people's responses.

Kim: What time is it in my life? At some times my attitude would suggest that it's very late. Or that it's at least one-half past the beginning—and since the first half hasn't seen much fruit, there's discouragement about anything happening in the second half. That's considering time as chronology.

It's time to start. . . . What is it time to start doing? Well, it's late enough that if I don't start taking action, more years will pass. I'm sort of stuck here. I preach about the biblical call to reach out, but I am frightened to begin. I'm so easily trapped by legalism and I make everything into a legalistic trap.

It's time I got my act together. It's time I finished some things. Maybe it's, most of all, time to ease up on myself in some ways, but seek out the courage to take steps of self-discovery. Fear is a hindrance. And yet I must respect and accept some of the fears I have.

It's time I learned how to be properly interdependent with others and dependent on God. It's time to discover who I am. And to be satisfied with that person. And not to seek in others the acceptance that will give me validation.

I don't want to pretend here. This is written for me.

Brad: Right now I can't seem to find an appropriate time metaphor for my life. Maybe it's like waking up in the middle of the night when it's too dark to see my watch or a clock. I don't know what time it is. What *do* I know? Well, I'm awake, or maybe I'm dreaming, so at least that must mean I'm alive. This must be the night that the Lord has made, so I should rejoice and be glad in it. O.K., I'm glad I'm alive. Now, should I get up or go back to sleep? If it's nearly dawn I might as well get up and get some work done while it's quiet, before the phone rings. If it's the middle of the night, I should try to fall

"In journaling we are taking care of things inside, so that we can be more Christ-like, better servants."

asleep again. Maybe I'll just see if I can get back to sleep. If so, I needed the rest. If not, I'll know I should get up. I should start listening to my own rhythm, maybe, and pay less attention to other people's schedules and deadlines.

Sirpa: It feels as if I'm in the middle. In a way I'd like to prolong youth, the youth I didn't have for so long, childhood that escaped me—and the crazy idea of having another baby, giving birth one more time, smelling the hair of a newborn, nursing—feeling young one more time. On the other hand, our children are so capable; we can leave them with the oldest and go out. On the beach I can close my eyes. No one's going to drown: no toddler suddenly running into the water.

Choices. Should I seek a permanent position? Could I go back to school? Is it still possible to get my Ph.D.? Or should I just enjoy life? Is it time to have time for workshops like this? Is it time to help people in a real way, make my faith real? Should I just calmly enter into middle-age with my husband? Is it time for routine—when I'm still seeking excitement and fulfillment?

Can God really guide me to find answers? How do I tell his answers from the advice given by well-meaning, culturally bound American Christian women?

Lorna: I'm supposed to be experiencing mid-life crisis, and maybe I am without realizing it. Something within me says, "If you're going to do something else, you'd better get on with it." I'm not really feeling panicky, just slightly uncomfortable because I have always known before just what I wanted to do next. I like security. I am really glad to be at the point in life where I don't have to worry about "the competition." Forty is much more satisfying than twenty-six. I know I have abilities, I know I can provide sufficiently for myself, I know I can accept singleness, and I know that God gives me worth. But one thing I don't know, and that is what comes next.

Alice: It's nine p.m. I'm three-fourths of the way to the end. I feel so much urgency. I need time to become all the things I've postponed becoming. And I need to realize I won't become all that because it's so late.

Maybe we're through with our mid-life crisis when we're ready to accept our limitations.

It's also springtime in my life because of the new hopes and dreams and ambitions bursting to be expressed. It's not second childhood—it's second adolescence!

It's endtime in the sense of looking back and discovering the meaning of my life's course.

And it's looking-ahead time, too. What is my spiritual course to be? I seem to focus so much, now, on the spiritual. Yet I can't leave the temporal: my livelihood, my household, my parenting. And now, grandparenting.

Lissa: At thirty-five, I'm frightened of aging and the downhill side of my life. The clock says it should be nearing six o'clock, the evening setting in, with night approaching. But I fight against it, wanting to turn the hands back to give me more time. I cannot see or hear in darkness. I'm afraid of the dark.

But if I look at it the other way—that six o'clock is just after dawn, the awakening of heart and soul, the approaching of more light, more understanding—that I can do, with joy, anticipation, and less caution. The dawning of a day fresh and alive with possibilities. New choices. Nothing decided yet.

So I must choose which it will be: the end of my day and approaching darkness, or the beginning of my day and approaching light.

Making Lists   A second writing exercise about time consists of making four lists, each on a separate sheet of notebook paper, dated, with these titles:

It is too late to . . .
It is too soon to . . .
The time is right to . . .
I need time to . . .

What thoughts come to your mind under each phrase? Jot down your answers briefly and quickly, just to see what this kind of brainstorming brings up. Feel free to jump from one page to another. Later on, you can write more extensively about any answers that need further exploration.

Here are some individual responses to those four phrases. Yours will be different but more important to you—because they are yours.

Janet: It is too late to . . .
   re-live my high school and college years
   re-live the early years with our kids
   talk more to my mother
   try to talk more humanly with my father
   start studying Russian this semester

Faye: It is too soon to . . .
   settle into a staid old age
   think nothing good is ahead and there's nothing to look
      forward to
   say we'll never get back to Europe
   think I'll never get organized

Kim: The time is right to . . .
   get my hands on wood: cutting, gluing, sanding, smooth-
      ing, creating
   walk and listen and feel God's wind (his promise of his pres-
      ence with me)
   see the possibility of a lean, fit body, disciplined by right
      diet and exercise
   count the cost of following Jesus

Lynn: I need time to . . .
do nothing
reflect, relax, pray, play
listen, respond
study the Bible, think, cry

Kim: I need time to . . .
organize my room
read and reflect
be with friends; so many are so busy, and it's hard to try to mesh our schedules. Something's wrong here. I don't want my life to be like that.

Answering Questions

Another exercise related to time is sometimes used in time-management seminars. Get out three sheets of paper, add today's date, and title the pages with the following questions:

What do I want to accomplish in my life?
What do I want to accomplish in the next three years?
What would I do if I had only six months to live?

Again, write only brief answers to these questions. Here are two responses:

June: What do I want to accomplish in my life? I want to write voluminously. In this, I want (high pretension!) to serve God, heal persons, make God and people laugh.

What do I want to accomplish in the next three years? I want to fill many, many pages, throw away nearly as many as I fill, make great headway in my writer's apprenticeship. I want to steer clear of romantic entanglements, the better to know myself. I want to publish, but only what's good enough to be published. I want to paint my kitchen and bathroom. I want to grow closer to those to whom I am closest.

If I had six months to live? God knows, God knows. Seek reconciliation with persons, with myself. Try to say the things I've "always wanted to say." Take a real good look at the things I forget to see. Spend a lot of hours at the sea. Maybe write a perfect sonnet. A sonnet for each person I love—And why not?

Sam: What do I want to accomplish? I don't know how to answer this. Should it be phrased, "What does the Lord want me to accomplish in life—to do with the rest of my life?" I want:

to do justice (do what is right)
to love mercy (be kind)
to walk humbly with God (live in a spirit of faith and trust)
to learn more Greek
to learn more Hebrew

"I realized the beauty of all the people's words in listening to what they had written; everything sounded like poetry. Bringing one's honesty into words is a dazzling process."

I want to be wise. Am I always looking for the "crystallizing thought"? Am I trying to "capture life in a few axioms," as one writer said? Is that why I want more schooling? But does more schooling make one wise?

I'd like to travel more (review German, learn more French).

What about the next three years? Could I write a book? I've been thinking about that for a long time.

What if I had six months to live? Certainly I'd work on my relationship with God; I'd try to do faith-enhancing study.

Take another sheet of paper, title it "Inner Country," and date it with today's date. Then ask yourself: Who are the people in my Inner Country? What does this metaphor imply? Which persons do I think about, or care about, most these days? What is the most important thing happening in the lives of these people, or in my relationship with them, that concerns me?

Your Inner Country

List the initials or names of three, or four, or five of them
and then ask yourself what you would especially like to say to
each one—if you could be completely open and honest.
Remember, an individual doesn't have to be geographically
close, or even still living, to be a resident of your Inner Country. For this exercise, write a brief note to each of these individuals, but only a couple of sentences for now. (Later you can
develop more fully the ideas that come up.)

These are examples of the notes that two people wrote to
inmates of their Inner Country. (Here, as in other places in this
book, some of the names and initials are pseudonymous.)

Anne: To AB: I want you to enjoy your life and do with it
what you want. I wish you liked me more, or expressed it, or
showed it by wanting to spend time with me. I wish I felt safe
with you.

To CD: I don't want to feed your cynicism. I want you to be
successful as a writer. I don't always know how much to say
to you, since you don't need another mother.

To EF: You're special because you're so sensitive and open
and sincere. I don't want people to hurt you. I want you to find
your place in life—and a loving husband. Thank you for liking me.

To GH: Oh, GH, I feel so bad for you. I know what "betrayal"
by a spouse feels like—even though my circumstances were
different. I want to empathize and give you my support. You're
such a remarkable person; I'm sad to see these days being so
hard on you.

To IJ: I'm fed up with your dishonesty and promiscuity—
that you're not concerned to be continent, and clean up your
life and be a Christian witness. I don't want always to look at
you judgingly, but can't you see you're cutting off contacts
with Christian men who *are* concerned to please God in their
behavior?

Pat: To Twink: Your presence and joy are helping me love the "Pat" that God intends me to be.

To Norm: I release you, my friend, my love, to walk away from me—back to your predictable world. I continue to love you and miss you though.

To Carolyn: You have always been there for me: my good friend—sensitive, insightful, caring.

To Doug: We have come full circle, you and I—very nearly back to the warm and tender acceptance we began with in our relationship fifteen years ago. I am starting to reach out ever so tentatively and to trust you again.

Note: All the writing you do for these four exercises, now and later, can be filed under the first notebook divider, *Who Am I?*

---

1. Who Am I?
2. My Days
3. Turning Points
4. Present Tense
5. Free-Flow Writing
6. Affirmations
7. Unsent Letters
8. Conversations
9. Conversations with God (or Jesus)

Suggested Titles for Nine Notebook Dividers

Just As I Am helps you start journal writing in the above nine categories. Gradually, though, you may become aware of topics you're writing about, or want to write about, that do not fit neatly into any of these areas. A great benefit of loose-leaf journaling is that you can then add new notebook dividers for the other kinds of writing that spring out of your own background and experience.

Here are some divider categories that other journal-keepers have found helpful to add to their journals:

Bible Notes (insights from Bible study)
Prayers (written out)
Good Memories
Things I've Written (poetry, etc.)
Poems I Like
Quotes from My Reading (add your response)
Connections (insights "out of the blue")
Letters to Myself (e.g., written on December 31 to be sealed up and read a year later)
My Children
Family Lore
Current Events (your response to happenings in the world around you)
Goals/Lists (ideas to act on)
Our Trip to _____
Dream-Catching

You will soon discover that there's always more to say.

To Number My Days 3

To write some kind of daily account in your journal may at first sound fairly easy. It's the kind of diary writing a lot of people do—for awhile. But then, you know how it goes. Life gets busy for one reason or another. You have too much homework, the laundry needs doing, you're too tired after your job, there's a foot-high stack of unanswered mail, the kids wear you out. "I hardly ever sit still without being haunted by the 'undone' and the 'unsent,'" wrote May Sarton in one of my favorite books.[1] And so, journal-writing momentum comes to an end.

Sometime later, perhaps at the beginning of a new year, or on your birthday, or because of some other major event, you hunt up your journal and resume—with regrets that so much of life has again passed you by. A new cycle begins.

Other factors, too, can cause us to stop writing. One day isn't all that different from another. Before long we start hearing a silent voice inside telling us that this is really pointless. What we write is so ordinary, so prosaic, so pedestrian. Why bother?

Even professional writers know that feeling. Poet Luci Shaw writes: "Each of us has within us . . . an Internal Critic, or Internal Censor, who tells us that our writing is idiotic, badly expressed, trivial . . . we have nothing to say, and we're wasting our time trying to write anything."[2]

The experience of a creative writing teacher was similar. He wasn't just off in the clouds abstractly theorizing when he said: "Maybe you don't like your [writing] voice; maybe people have made fun of it. But it's the only voice you've got. . . . If you keep writing in it, it may change into something you like better. But if you abandon it . . ."[3] *Zilch.*

You Have to Choose

Writing in your journal is a choice. Of course there is always something more important for you to be doing, or so says that insidious inside voice. If you pay attention to that voice, and obey it, submitting to its dark clobbering of your journaling aspirations, you will once again set your notebook aside in discouragement.

This isn't to say that in order to succeed at journal-keeping you have to be fanatic about it. The pendulum can swing that way, too. Even though you do write from time to time, there may arise a haunting voice that berates you for your negligence in keeping your journal up-to-date. You are a victim of that legalistic compulsion I mentioned in chapter 1.

Rather, I want to stress one point. Journaling is a tool to use when you need it. The longer you keep a journal, the more convinced you will probably become that it's a helpful tool in sorting out your life, understanding what's going on, clarifying current priorities, and drawing you closer to God. In my experience, when I see all the people around me who want attention or need help, and I know my own inadequacies, limited energy, and need for wisdom, I am more apt to turn to the one who can cope with the day's (and the world's) problems in a way that I can't. "Once we establish a trust relationship to the journal and ourselves, and are comfortable with writing, the journal begins to act as a partner in the process of working through our limitations."[4]

So, what are you doing with your days? To be specific, what has your *today* been like? Will you choose to write in your journal today? One journal writer described having a dream in which a wise person spoke these words: "The days become months, and the months become years, and that is the pattern."[5]

A few weeks ago the oldest of my first cousins died. Remembering my few encounters with her, I began thinking about family history and how little my sisters and I know of it. I got out an old family Bible printed in Stuttgart, Germany, an 1886 copy of *Die Heilige Schrift* that I inherited from my father. Slowly I began deciphering the names written in that old German script. The entries began with the marriage of my paternal grandparents, and then one by one listed the births of their nine children over the next decade. My father was child number seven. Three of those children died in infancy.

In the back of that Bible, I found a picture of my paternal grandmother's parents, along with their dates of birth, marriage, and death. That was all. What was she like, my grandmother Katherine, growing up in nineteenth-century Germany? What were her parents, Georg Christof and Margarethe, like? Were they people of faith? What had they done with their days? Did my grandmother have brothers and sisters? What a wonderful thing it would have been if my great-grandparents, or their daughter Katherine, or one of her children (perhaps Gottlob, my father), had kept a diary now preserved along with those few long-ago dates in the fragile pages of *Die Heilige Schrift*.

Start Now

"Teach me, O Lord," the psalmist said, "to number my days, that I may apply my heart to wisdom" (paraphrase of Ps. 90:12). To help you do that, starting now, label your second notebook divider *My Days*. Each page in this section will be dated (of course) and titled "Today." What you write here will resemble a daily diary somewhat, but there will be important differences.

In this journal, the idea is not to make a laundry list of the day's events. "Today" is not intended to be a tabulation or

"My writing has contributed to my sense of myself as God's person in process."

chronicle of your activities. (Who has time on most evenings for that?) Remember, you are not failing as a journal-keeper if you don't write "Today" every day. Rather, try to write when you can reasonably fit it into your day's-end schedule.

Begin, as usual, by taking a few minutes to "center." Then ask yourself questions like these: What was most important about this day? How did I respond to it? What was I most concerned with? Was anything consciously bothering me? Did I have any awareness of God's hand on my life? Did I try to acknowledge him in all or even some of my ways (Prov. 3:6)?

Don't try to analyze the day's events. Instead, let them rise naturally in your mind. After taking those few minutes to calm down, pick up your pen and start to write—aiming more for a stream-of-consciousness type of writing than a formal, well-organized recapitulation. Let your memories lead you where they will. Your thoughts may take unexpected twists and turns. Sometimes the path they choose will amaze you. You may see new connections. You may find yourself praying. That's great. But keep on writing.

Give yourself ten or fifteen minutes, not much more than that, to write "Today." Then file it under the second divider in your journal notebook.

Here are several examples of what people have written in this category.

Kitt: A day full of feelings, discoveries, questions, hopes. The allergy testing today was good and bad. I don't want to be allergic to anything. I fear being allergic to things like grass. I like the outdoors, pretty manicured lawns, to take walks in the hills, to play golf. I don't want to be afraid to do these things, yet I would like to know why my body gets upset.

But maybe knowing what causes my unhappy body will make it better—easier to control, to accept. God, help me to know and accept my limitations, but also not to place unnecessary limitations imposed by others or by my own fear.

It's hard to commit so much to paper. I write so slowly, but my mind goes so fast.

This "hay fever" is getting to me. I'm tired of it. I'm forgetting what a good night's sleep is like. Oh, just to sleep until I'm no longer tired. I'm also tired of having a weird body. Lord, are you teaching me here, too? Help me to learn your lessons.

Russell: I felt good about running this morning, feeling that I've probably gotten back in the habit now, able to run two miles even when I don't think I'll make it because I'm too stiff when I get up. I felt good about making a journal entry after missing almost a month, realizing how much more lasting my work with my hands seems when I record it. Otherwise, though, I felt defeated at not concentrating on the tasks at hand, i.e., cleaning off the pile on my desk and taking care of each thing as I came to it. Was I even thinking very clearly about what to do? Is my focus so diffuse now that I'm finding it hard to get anything done?

Sirpa: Friday. What an odd day. Getting up at night again and again, cleaning up after my six-year-old with stomach flu. Mountains of sheets and pillow cases in the bathtub; she wakes up one more time at four a.m.

Exhausted after a party and dinner in the city, I get up and fall asleep again. At seven a.m. I run to the bathroom—now I've got it too. All the children are sick, to varying degrees. We lie in bed, sleep, read, drink tea.

The mail brought a 48-hour notice about the gas and electric bill. I drag myself out of bed, shower, take my son along as a messenger. I drive to pay the bill, buy soda—which is supposed to help. I return to reading a book; I move to lie down on the lawn. Someone wants dinner. I have a piece of toast. Odd day—for my first journal workshop.

Saturday. I feel so alive; thank you, Lord, for healing me. What a joy to feel my strength returning. What a joy to be able to eat. So many things in life I take for granted. Thank you, Lord, for the sick day. I needed it to be able to appreciate the healthy days.

Sunday. It was a full day, a fulfilled day. We wrote . . . images coming from deep inside, memories from the far past. It was a dream day for me, having hours in the sun, with just paper and pen—a self-centered day; I haven't had many of them for years. It was a day worth more than many visits to a counselor, a healing day, an honest day, living out a side of me that few people know: a quiet, inward, reflective side. Days like this I need more of, many more.

Note: File your "Today" writing, now and in the future, under the second notebook divider, *My Days.*

After being in the workshop, at my request *Alice* sent me a poem she had written about one of her days. She called it "Monday Morning."

> Monday Morning
>
> Awake at five.
> Talk to me, Lord.
>
> If a word came
> even edgewise
> I didn't hear it.
> Brain into automatic
> rehash the past/plan today.
>
> Downstairs.
> The dog has peed again
> in the kitchen.
> (I don't need this!)
> I kneel (not in prayer),
> use half a towel roll to mop up.
>
> Brain screen flashes
> yesterday's news:

Iowa neighbors pass sandbags
by the Mississippi.
Beyond mopping, they wade in their kitchens.

A whine of distress.
Blind Becky can't find the back steps.
(I need to get dressed!)
Down the steps, guide her up.
Rub salve on her dermatitis.
(Yuk! How long, God,
will this old dog live?)

More brain screen channels:
My sister Edith tends her aging friend,
changing her diapers.
Nurse-friend Kate helps a Berkeley vagrant
in a hospital shower,
cutting his matted hair,
easing dirt crusts from his skin.

And I recoil from bumps on a dog's back.

God's word slides in edgewise,
something about doing
for the least of these and
"Do you love me, Alice?
Feed my dog!"

                    Alice Macondray

Looking Backwards 4

Chapter 3 asked: What are you doing with your days? Now this question broadens to: What are you doing with your life? Is it what you want to be doing? Those questions are not always easy to answer.

Because contemporary American life tends to leave us overly busy, we often lose touch with our inner being. True, we may be fulfilling our daily responsibilities, but sometimes it is in a semi-numb or half-awake state. We do the next thing, and the next, and the next. We forget the overall goals we once had set for ourselves—even what our most recent New Year's resolutions were. We forget to pray. Hearing that old adage, "Those who forget the past are doomed to repeat it," we may experience a vague disquiet.

That is why our third journaling category looks back at the turning points of our life. It is important to be clear about what has really been happening over the years. Because certain experiences remain with us, consciously or unconsciously, we need to be aware of those determinative life "markers."

I suggest labeling the third divider in your journal notebook *Turning Points.*[1]

To write down your own life's turning points will help you gain perspective. It will let you see what some of your personal milestones have been—times when a particular event or decision resulted in a major shift in your thinking, experience, and/or direction. At the time, of course, you may not have realized the significance of what was happening, but now in retrospect, as you write, you can see the impact it had. Whatever recollections come up (when you are not forcing them into awareness) probably do have a bearing on your present. They show the direction your life is moving. The *Turning Points* exercise helps you integrate those past experiences more consciously into your present and future.

Where to Begin

To begin, write today's date on a clean sheet of paper and title it "My Turning Points." Then take a few minutes to be quiet. Try to set aside temporarily whatever analytical tendencies you have; instead, allow the general course of your life to come into your awareness. What turning points from your past come to mind? Since the following event fits everybody, it is an easy place to start: 1. I was born.

Moving on from that remarkable occurrence, what else should be on your list? What happenings or developments seem to have influenced the person you now are? Do a relatively quick itemizing of these things, and don't worry if you remember them in the wrong order. You can always renumber your list, or draw arrows to relocate its notations more accurately. If you think of yourself as young, try to list no more than ten. If you are very young, fewer are okay. If you are older, limit yourself to twelve.

An interesting result of doing this exercise more than once, perhaps repeating it six months or a year later, is that some of your turning points will vary. Different memories come up. "What our past means at any given time is always conditioned by the present questions we bring to it."[2] As we move on in life, events from earlier years take on different meanings. Things that once seemed crucial may change with time. New interpretations of past experiences can also arise to affect the present.

Here is a list written by *Walt*, a repeater in the journal workshop.

1. Born
2. Christian commitment
3. Career choice
4. Professional associations
5. Writing for publication
6. Marriage
7. Thinking and writing about lifestyle and goals
8. Cross-country move
9. Book contract
10. This workshop

Walt read his list and wrote a response. He noted the element of choice as one characteristic of his turning points (except number 1). He also realized that all except number 3 were continuing commitments (though number 3 had influenced the later ones), and he asked himself if the list he had written was perhaps skewed by his current commitments.

In a later workshop, Walt's list went like this:

1. I was born; and then reborn as a child of God
2. I survived childhood diseases
3. I survived sibling rivalry
4. I survived puberty, high school
5. I survived college and grad school competition
6. I survived World War II
7. I survived marriage and divorce
8. I survived years with teenage kids
9. I survived a change in careers at age 45
10. I survived skin cancer and an emergency airplane landing
11. I survived challenges to my faith in Christ
12. I have survived all sorts of controversies

After rereading his list, Walt wrote this response: That's quite a bit of survival. Why should I worry about what the future might hold? My life has been in God's hands all this time. I can trust him.

After listing your own turning points, take a minute to look them over. Each turning point was a hub of events and opportunities. Do they stir up any strong feelings? Are there significant omissions? Surprises? Do you see themes or patterns? Do they have present-tense consequences? Any other observations? Write down anything along these lines that you see in your list. You will soon discover that rereading and then writing a response are important parts of journal-keeping.

Life Themes

Another approach to writing in the Turning Points category is to focus on experiences that relate to a particular theme. Here are some possibilities:

Surprises	Best friends/special people
Early memories	Major decisions
Separations/loss	Dramatic events
Other people's expectations of me	Mistakes
My expectations	Lessons learned
Fears	Deliverances
Feeling powerless, left out, deprived	Victories
Relationships with others, parents	Defeats
Celebrations/ holidays/"rituals"	My children's lives
Circumstances forced on me	

Any of your entries in this category can be explored more fully in further journal-writing. Each one may lead to new insights. Each one, as Thomas Merton described it, can become a "seed of contemplation." Each entry has redemptive potential as you gradually come to realize God's hand on your life.

Spiritual Milestones

Another list of turning points may be related to spiritual milestones. (Some may already have appeared on your earlier lists.) Take a new sheet of paper, date it with today's date, and label it "My Spiritual Turning Points."

All of us go through a lifelong process of spiritual evolution, whether or not our families of birth were in any sense religious. Some were taken to church every Sunday from the time they were a few weeks old. Others didn't come into contact with formal religion, or with basic Christianity, until they were much older—and then it may have happened away from, or in spite of, family influence. But from the time we were very young, we all have had special times of spiritual awareness.

To begin this writing, ask yourself questions like these: When was I first aware of an important reality or power beyond myself? Under what circumstances did I have some kind of sensitivity to God? Did something that was said suddenly hit me hard spiritually? Did a scene in a movie or a passage in a book speak to me about ultimate concerns? Did a Bible verse I heard or read stay with me and start to make sense? Did I have a friend whose religious convictions mystified or intrigued me?

"It seems so simple, just writing, but it can be a deep experience of connection with one's self and with God."

Southern Catholic writer Flannery O'Connor called such experiences "moments of grace" and she tried to portray them in her writing: "There is a moment of grace in most of [my] stories, or a moment where it is offered, and is usually rejected . . . I am interested in the indication of Grace, the moment when you know that Grace has been offered and accepted. . . ."[3]

Can you think of moments of grace in your life? One of your spiritual turning points, or spiritual milestones (though probably not the first one), may have been when you began to understand who Jesus was, why he came to earth, and what that meant for *you.* You may say it was then that you "accepted Christ," or "became a Christian," or were "born again." Perhaps, like C. S. Lewis, you found yourself "surprised by joy."

Perhaps other experiences gradually and cumulatively caused you to grow into a personal faith that now sustains you. What were those experiences? Take time now to try to write down some of your spiritual turning points.

Lois's list had sixteen entries. Here are the first seven, which perhaps played a role in her eventual Christian commitment.

1. Sensitivity in Sunday school songs to the name of Jesus; not wanting to sing it.
2. Being at my uncle's on my first vacation (age ten) and waking up cold at night. Awake there in the dark I became aware of endlessness (how could there be an end to the universe, and if there was, what was beyond that?) and the possibility of my own death. I was afraid.
3. Church camp, where I felt aware of God when I looked at the stars in the night sky, and decided I wanted to live for him.
4. My idealism as a senior in high school; having a strong, longing response toward the good, the ethical.
5. Going into open churches to pray (about *what* I wonder now) when I was a college freshman, and not knowing how to distinguish between Christianity and Judaism when I talked with others in my dorm.
6. Sneering at my boyfriend's childishness when he said about Jesus, "He died for us, didn't he?"
7. A few months later, understanding that no one "makes it" to heaven by good behavior and that God has forgiven our sins through Jesus if we are willing to accept his forgiveness. I was willing—and I felt a lot of relief that it wasn't all up to me.

Rather than making a list of her spiritual turning points, *Carol* wrote the following description:

Having been brought up in the Church of Christ in East Texas, I took on the conservative attitudes of the adults in my world from the time I was baptized into Christ at the age of twelve. Though I knew what I was doing and that it was required if I wanted to call myself a Christian, I didn't understand the concept of grace or forgiveness past my parents' forgiving me for my occasional misjudgments. My teenage years were spent dealing with a woman's body housing a nun's conscience and attending school dances but refusing to dance because it would send me straight to hell.

My first marriage resulted in three children by a handsome and talented young man with no guts and no faith. I struggled alone in my church attendance for nine years, while my children were young, all the while resenting him for not helping me and wondering if that was what God really wanted from me.

After a few years of nothingness following our divorce, Mell came into my life and I discovered God again. Only this time it was fun. I never knew that being a Christian could be so rewarding. Life was wonderful. Then Mell died and I was mad at God. When I went back to church the week after he died, I hated all the happy little families with fathers, especially when the father and mother held hands and prayed together. After two years, I did not go back.

But I didn't lose sight of God, and he certainly did not turn his back on me. In spite of my nonattendance at the fellowship of Christians where I had been serving, I somehow did not feel I was missing anything. That was 1983. Since then, three people have called or contacted me once each about our absence. Now when I occasionally visit, I am welcomed much as a visitor but with genuine warmth. I cannot understand how I can refuse to go to church and still say I love Jesus.

"It is good to have a place to put things and thoughts in an organized fashion. Before, my journal was only for 'grumblings' to myself."

I know that God hears me when I pray, and I know he answers my prayers. He is in my life and in the lives of my children. This is a transition I do not understand and one with which I will struggle for a long time, I am sure.

The next Turning Point is not in sight.

Chris also chose to write about her spiritual background in a few paragraphs. This is what she wrote:

In my childhood days, I served a "benign grandfather-in-the-sky God." Someone who was always there, like Mother, to kiss skinned knees and pat me on the head when things seemed rough. That slowly changed during the next several years, and by the time I entered high school, he had become the "gimme God." "Give me what I want or else, God" (in typical demanding adolescent fashion). "You owe it to me; it's my right to have this," etc.

In college, I took part in a religious group that again changed my view of God. My image of him during that time became one of a stern, rigid, paternalistic watchdog who would turn on me at the blink of an eye, the moment I stepped out of line. He was the "celestial bogeyman," a divine law enforcement agent. But I thank God for the time when I finally realized that such a theology was sadly and inherently lacking in love, and I moved away from it.

In the last five years, after reaching my mid-twenties, little seeds of Grace have blown my way, coming on the gentle yet insistent breeze of the Holy Spirit (no wind is sweeter) and now I serve a laughing, dancing God—one who *joys* in the gifts he gives to his children. I delight in the knowledge that he has in store for me only what will lead to my greatest good: my growing in love and understanding of Who He Is.

A man who has kept a journal for many years wrote these words in one of the earliest Christian books about journal-keeping:

There is only one way I know of to have confidence that my value goes beyond this moment and continues in the life to come: coming to know and experience the incredible love of the heavenly Father who has created this universe, both spiritual and physical, and still holds it in his hand. A journal helps us toward this realization and is also a record of our unique experience of this love.[4]

Note: File the writing you do in this category under the third notebook divider, *Turning Points*.

Taking the Next Step

Part 2

We are important and our lives are important, magnificent really, and their details are worthy to be recorded. This is how [journal] writers must think, this is how we must sit down with pen in hand. . . . Our details are important.

Natalie Goldberg
Writing Down the Bones

There is no event so commonplace but that God is present within it, always hiddenly, always leaving you room to recognize him or not to recognize him, but all the more fascinatingly because of that, all the more compellingly and hauntingly.

Frederick Buechner
Now & Then: A Memoir of Vocation

Chapter (and Verse) 5

All of us go through various phases—you might say chapters—in our lives, but without reflection we may be unaware of what those phases or chapters have been. If you are just beginning to keep a journal, or if you have not written in yours for awhile, it helps to take a present-tense look at the chapter you are in right now. Therefore a new category in your journal should be devoted to this kind of writing. Let's call the fourth notebook divider *Present Tense*.[1]

Writing the Present Tense exercise will give you a broad overview of your life. It's a way to anchor yourself in the present, as distinct from your past and your future. Your Present Tense chapter will probably have many dimensions (let's say many verses) and it will take more than a few minutes to write.

The way to start is to ask yourself: When did this present chapter, or phase, of my life begin? It may have begun last week, when you decided to keep a journal. It may have begun last month, when you moved into a new house or apartment. It may have begun in January, when you first went to AA or changed jobs. Maybe it began two years ago when you got married or were divorced or remarried, or when your youngest child started preschool or your only daughter went off to college.

Try to think of some event that sets off this current chapter of your life from the time before it. What circumstances led up to it? In writing this exercise, try to explore your present life from as many vantage points as possible. These are some areas you might choose to cover:

- What are you doing with your life right now (commitments, job, school, projects)?
- What relationships are important to you? (You got a start on this one before, if you wrote the "Inner Country" notes in chapter 2.)
- What about your health? What's going on with your body these days?
- What ties to society do you have? What organizations or social groups are you in?
- Have there been high points, low points? Puzzling events? Testings, disappointments? Unexpected developments?
- Is anything happening in your life that would surprise other people if they knew about it?
- What about your relationship with God? What is your spiritual experience these days?
- What lies ahead? Where do you anticipate that this chapter of your life will lead? Where would you like it to lead?

To get started, try to think of a simile or metaphor that characterizes this time of your life: This chapter of my life is like _____. Does that phrase bring up any image or picture? If so, you can begin your writing with that sentence.

It is not necessary to answer all of the above questions. Rather, start with any one of them and see where your thoughts take you next. Be honest. Be specific. Write down any feelings that your writing stirs up.

Because this exercise sometimes brings surprising, even powerful similes or metaphors to people's minds, it is always inspiring to have some of the workshop participants tell what their images were. For one person, life was like walking down a lonely country road. Someone else mentioned being lost in the woods. Another person felt it was like standing on the edge of a high diving board poised to jump. One man said his life was like driving on the freeway during five o'clock rush hour. Another person described it as being suspended in the calm eye of a hurricane. Others have chosen metaphors like clearing away underbrush, building a cabin in the woods, planting a garden, being "on call" or on guard duty in the military, starting off on a "mission," working in a very busy store at Christmas time, preparing for a trip, getting ready for final exams, walking a tightrope with balance pole in hand, and so on.

Meredith wrote about the trauma her family was experiencing right then over a wayward son:

The metaphor of a boomerang comes to mind. This chapter of my (our) life began when Travis, age twenty-eight, moved back home—at first grateful and responsive, and then (in about ten days, when faced with having to get a job and begin supporting himself) withdrawn, angry, pouting—reminiscent of his behavior half his lifetime ago at age fourteen, and even before that.

By age seven, Travis was rebelling in various ways; for three-quarters of his life he has been a rebel. Last night I was counting up the major times we've tried to help him "get a fresh start." There have been more than twelve—and each time he has turned toward wrongdoing. He has "lived for a lie," as he himself described it last Sunday morning after a dream-induced, short-lived "repentance."

But by Monday he had disappeared and evidently he eventually took a bunch of sleeping pills. Sometime that afternoon the police found him lying face down somewhere, and he was taken to the emergency room of the county hospital. We didn't know what had happened (as a juvenile he had a pattern of running away) until he called us at seven a.m. two days later, wanting David (his father) to "get him out." The powers-that-be would let him go, he said, if we would guarantee him a place (room, food, and payment of his hospital expenses).

We had invited him to come with us to this workshop—and he seemed interested. But that possibility evaporated when he took off, split, at the beginning of the week.

Travis clearly isn't "good for" us. As an adult his behavior is still interruptive and disruptive. All our efforts to help him over the years have come to naught; he cancels them, or undermines them in some way. Yet we have always wanted "the good" for him. We have always wanted to do our best by him. We have prayed for grace and wisdom, love, understanding, and kindness in dealing with him. But *all comes to naught.*

Now, Lord, what? Please lead us; help us know what to do. We look to your Spirit to convince Travis of "sin and righteousness and judgment." Open up your way for him, for us. No one can be helped unless they want help. David and I *again* want your help: wisdom, strength, grace. *Now.*

Outwardly David and I are calm—thinking that Travis has already hurt us so much, disappointed us so often, that he can hardly hurt us more. Inwardly we are—witness what I am writing this exercise about—very stirred up and troubled.

The other day David asked, "If Travis is adamant in 'choosing death,' does it matter if he dies sooner than later?"

If there's life, is there hope?

After difficult years with young children and marital strain, *Nancy* wrote about hope and new patterns:

This chapter of my life began when things with Scott began to go not so badly, when there was a relaxing about who we are together. Timewise it coincided with Teddy's enrollment in preschool.

My commitments are to God—one "has to" put him first (God, Lord, free me from this compulsive legalism). But in my heart of hearts it is still true: You, God, are in and over and around and through the whole of my life and I want it this way and it is this way and You are God and I rest in Your love. A good place to start.

Then there is my marriage and on that score I say, "Okay, Scott, your turn to take up the slack." So really my commitments are to the children, Todd, Elizabeth, and Teddy. What I do with them is probably most important of all. And there is no time to lose.

For Todd—I want to be a container (one of many) for his discoveries. I hope for him to enjoy life, to be good enough at sports not to feel bad, and to learn to love: to be kind and caring.

For Elizabeth—things are so good and close between us now, after such conflict when she was three to six years old. I want to offer her some of the "feminine," helping her with clothes and hair, while also encouraging her in sports and school.

"Even the 'difficult' writing stretches me."

For Ted—to play. My last chance to play with him, at least as a little guy. May I really do it, Lord. Play is healing for me and an essential building block for him.

No big events are happening right now, but I feel profound gratitude for the unexpected love coming my way from Scott after such struggles together—and for the energy newly freed up as a result of this peacefulness at last. I want this chapter to lead further into a happy, close family that includes Scott.

Karen, on vacation, was finally having time to think:

I'm at a lull now, as if white-water rapids had swirled into a broad place in the river and become still, before hurtling over rocks again. I'm so much in the *middle* of something, my third year of med school, that I'm tempted to call *that* the chapter, rather than these weeks of vacation.

I've hardly had time to experience what I've been doing. Everything was so new on the wards and moved so fast. So many things I'd never experienced before. Having a patient die the first week, having responsibility (however small) for the first time, working eighty hours a week, all night twice, dealing with people who were scared to death of their cancers, who were angry at life and at God because they were going to lose a breast or a foot—all these things I had never dealt with before. I didn't have time to feel anything, except to go home and dream terrifying dreams—it was the only way I could feel these things, in my sleep.

So far I've been writing more about the chapter *before* this one; these days are like a few paragraphs within it. What's behind and what's ahead are basically the same stuff, but this is completely separate. I'm in the middle of this weird metamorphosis, of becoming a doctor, and I want to look at what I'm doing and becoming. I don't want to become someone I don't want to be.

Sensing transition ahead, *Lorna* was concerned to wait on the Lord until his way for her was clear:

This phase of my life is like being in a blender on high speed while the ingredients are being combined. Ever since I was appointed three years ago this month to edit a Christian educators' quarterly journal, my focus has changed from the contentment and joy of reaching refreshingly crazy junior high kids to wanting something else. I have begun to experience positive feedback for expressing my opinions in my editorials, even though I am not, by nature, a confident person. So how did I get into this position? Opportunities like this have to be God-directed—I don't really expect them.

When I took on the editing job, I thought I would have no time for anything else, but I found the job to be a tremendous encouragement during the two roughest years of my teaching career. I had something positive to maintain my confidence during these difficult years, whereas my teaching colleagues did not.

That is when I realized I wanted to do something else besides teach junior high the rest of my working life. That's when I felt called to pursue a master's degree in order to be ready for whatever else God wants me to do in his service.

During this period I have become much more confident in making decisions about the magazine. I have also been mentally stimulated by the courses I have taken at the university near home and in England last summer. Every course I take seems to be the best one I have had, and each one inspires me to delve into a particular period of literature or aspect of writing. I get a little frustrated though, because I never get finished with one goal before I get into another course with another focus.

Lots of things in my life are unsettled right now. I have to decide soon whether to stay in my secure teaching job or to get into some other career. Can I accept the idea of teaching in a public education system when I am so committed to Christian education? Do I have to move in order to change careers? Can I adjust to leaving my sisters, my nephews, my community, my church, my home, my friends, my comfortable lifestyle? If I quit teaching in junior high, will I become distant from the people in my school community?

I am a woman with opinions, I am becoming a woman with confidence, I hope to be a woman with positive Christian influence in my community. But I want to be a humble woman. Sometimes I am surprised at what comes from my own mouth or my own pen. When people respond or react to my ideas, I wonder, "Now where did I get the guts to say that?" Then I wonder if they think I am too directive or too forceful with my ideas. Do I put distance between us because they think I have more answers?

Lots of people would say that I have my life all in order, but really, I'm still in the blender, on high speed. I don't even know how this new recipe will turn out. I only know that God supplies the ingredients, adding just the right amount.

Note: File the writing you do in this category under the fourth divider, *Present Tense.*

Silencing Your Editor 6

From time to time my husband and I have led writers' workshops. In the 1970s we did that through a Christian "free university" called The Crucible, one of the ministries of the Christian World Liberation Front. Anyone who wanted to teach a course could do so. The financial charge was minimal, usually five dollars or less. Anyone interested in writing was invited to come to our home one evening a week, read aloud from his or her own work, and listen to the writings of others. We team-taught that writers' workshop off and on for eight or nine years. At least one book by one of the participants in each of those workshops ended up being published.

We soon became aware of a problem, however. Some individuals, hearing about the writers' group, would come to read their writing aloud and to be heard by others. That is, they would come *once*. After they had been given a chance to read (they were always quick to volunteer), they never came back to listen and provide feedback to others who also wanted to read to an audience.

In the 1980s, after the founding of New College Berkeley, an offspring of The Crucible, our writers' workshop became a bit more formalized. Students actually signed up with the college registrar, paid a larger tuition fee, and had regular assignments to do at home in addition to their own major writing project. In those classes we emphasized the importance of students' learning to edit their own work.

But the best thing we did was introduce class members to what turned out to be a form of journal-keeping. We set aside the last fifteen minutes each evening for "free-flow writing." Students were asked to write, without stopping, anything that was on their mind or that came up as they wrote. We asked them to hand in their papers at the end of the time period, but said we would only read them; we would neither grade nor comment on them. For us as teachers it brought remarkable insight into our class members. Their free-flow writing enabled us to see what their lives were like outside our writers' workshop. Reading their unedited, uncensored thoughts gave us great empathy for each one of them and for their struggles as contemporary young adults. It helped us conduct our class more wisely and respond to each of them with greater sensitivity.

At the end of the course, we gave back to each student his or her packet of free-flow writings. The students were amazed at how much and how honestly they had written with so little effort. All it took was a few minutes of "enforced time" at the end of each class period to write. They got new confidence about how much they had to say. Several years later, one student wrote to tell us that of all the New College courses he took, the writers' workshop ended up being of greatest benefit to him when he finished his schooling.

Free-flow writing can be an effective journaling technique for almost anyone.

"It was a highlight to let 'inside knowledge' become 'outside knowledge' through pen and paper."

> Simply write for ten minutes. . . . Don't stop for anything. Go quickly without rushing. Never stop to look back, to cross something out, to wonder how to spell something, to wonder what word or thought to use, or to think about what you are doing. . . . The easiest thing is just to put down whatever is in your mind. . . . The only requirement is that you never stop. . . . The main thing about freewriting is that it is nonediting.[1]

Everyday journal-keeping has at least one of the advantages of free-flow writing. You are not graded on what you write. You don't have to worry about spelling, punctuation, or grammar. You don't have to be concerned with "style." It is not a place to flaunt your cleverness. It is not for the eyes of others.

Free-flow writing is so important that I suggest you give it a special category in your journal. Hunt up your notebook dividers and number the fifth one *Free-Flow Writing.* You can take a number of approaches to this writing, with any one of them apt to get you rather quickly into your present concerns. Free-flow writing can lead you to your "agenda," to what may be "out at the edge" but needs your attention.

The Spontaneous Approach

This is the exercise we used in the writers' workshop described above. Simply take a sheet of paper, date it (of course), and start writing nonstop for a fixed period of time. Then file what you have written in your journal notebook. Sometime later you can reread it with fresh eyes and consider just what is important about it.

The Springboard Approach

In this exercise you can use any word as a springboard for free-flow writing. This year, for example, I led one journaling group that met over a January weekend during California's rainy season. The host had set a basket of bright yellow daffodils on my worktable. The participants chose a word from the following list that I wrote on the board:

Rain	Quiet	Warm
Earthquake	Red	Daffodils
Fireplace	White	Music

After ten minutes of free-flow writing, many participants were willing to read aloud the thoughts that their word-choice had prompted. To hear what they had written was one of that workshop's high points. It gave everyone a chance to know the others in the group better. It showed all of us the value of free-flow writing.

In a later workshop, *Alice* chose to respond to the word "Quiet."

Quiet draws me at this point in my life. I live in a big city; the noise is constant. All day, voices—usually my students' voices in other languages, my own voice teaching. I get in the car, I turn on the radio, I cruise the dial. When I'm in the kitchen, I cruise the TV channels. I check on C-SPAN.

Yet often, at home, I don't want the TV or radio—not even baroque music. I want to listen to the quiet. I crave it.

At Echo Lake, sometimes I feel such an absence of sound that I make myself listen for birds, for a distant motor, for leaves whispering in a breeze.

Night quiet feels like a warm and comforting arm around me, a solid chest to lean against.

Quiet in the morning—I listen for God. I watch my thoughts and listen for them, in the quiet, to speak something profound. Something reassuring.

But quiet between people is hard for me. Why do we have nothing to say to each other?

Response to Something Visual

A journal workshop I attended as a participant was held in a large room with essentially no decorations. Bare walls. No furniture. Everyone, over a hundred people, sat on a large rug in the middle, or up against the walls. The first night the only journaling we did was to write for five minutes in a stream-of-consciousness style about something we could see in that room. We did that exercise three times. What could people possibly write about in a place so devoid of anything of interest? The leader sat on an ordinary stool a little higher than the group.

At her side was a small table with a pitcher of water and a glass.

Back at home, my cat Christopher was ill. In that stark setting, this is how my free-flow writing went:

> That pitcher of water reminds me of Christopher (maybe dying) who seemingly hasn't drunk water for days—and not enough for a long time. Walt and I have been hydrating him [subcutaneously] for about two years, two or three times a week, especially recently—and this last week every day, and now two times daily. Thank you, God, that we can do this—that Walt has had "needle experience" with rats in his years as a biochemist. Did I buy the last bottle of fluids, and venoset, and #18 needles from the vet today?
>
> We love Christopher so much, now twenty-one and a half years old. Amazing—today marks our twenty-year departure from Iowa for California with him and five other black cats in our VW Bug. (It must have been a bad year for all those people whose path we crossed!) Since Copy-cat's death in '86, Christopher has been our senior cat—sweet, docile, intelligent (even though he always looks so cross).

Everything I wrote that weekend tied into the Christopher theme. He died in the sunshine out on our deck about ten days later.

"Taking Off" from a Phrase

One writer has described what she calls "Timed Writing" exercises to help her get going on her current writing project.[2] She allots ten minutes to warm herself up with phrases like these:

I remember . . .	I don't remember . . .
I know . . .	I don't know . . .
I am . . .	I'm not . . .
I want . . .	I don't want . . .

Here are excerpts from what *Stephanie* wrote when she started doing free-flow writing in her journal.

I remember . . . how relaxing it was to hear the falling water from the garden hose one night last week when I was watering the herbs Robin set out in the backyard. This morning, as I sit here by the woodstove, I hear the water bubbling/boiling/brewing/stewing in the large old-time tea kettle from my parents' house.

"*Outer growth is so tangible; measuring inner growth requires a different yardstick. A journal is my 'inner yardstick.'*"

All that stuff from my childhood, right here in our living room and dining room: the dog-head chair, the mahogany table and chairs, the piano, the poplar hutch—and now Cedric and Karen have just taken my parents' china closet and server from the basement after all these years. Also here in the living room is my childhood wagon, painted red (at my request) by Jean-Claude for my Christmas present several years ago. Now it's lined with cardboard and we store wood in it.

Red. A word that brings to mind that William Carlos Williams poem about the red wheelbarrow, glazed by rain, with white chickens roaming near it. Its importance is in the poet's noticing, being aware. I want to pay attention to what is around me—and hear the voice of God's Spirit in my everydayness.

I don't remember . . . a lot of things about growing up in my parents' house, much less from when we lived with my grandmother before that. The red wagon dates back to that era—it was green then.

I don't remember much about school either, though seeing kids all over the streets at all hours now, I realize that school hours are shorter and procedures a lot looser. Polina, our adopted eighty-year-old *babushka* (Russian for "grandmother"), had her glasses pulled off and broken as she sat reading on her front steps the other day. Another friend, Rebecca, was hassled at three p.m. in front of the library by teenagers trying to steal her bike—even though Rebecca's two little kids were riding right there in the bike cart. Both these incidents took place right after the Rodney King verdict was announced. It isn't easy to live in a world where cruelty and "meanness" are so prevalent.

Giving yourself a start-up phrase, a few words to take off from, will help you move into free-flow journal writing should you find yourself stuck with nothing to say.

Ten minutes? Rather than be a clock-watcher, a distraction that can slow you down, I simply fill up one notebook-size sheet of college-ruled paper. When I get to the bottom line of the page, I know I'm through warming up and it's time to move on to the task at hand.

Note: File the writing you do in this category under the fifth notebook divider, *Free-Flow Writing.*

What I Believe and the Difference It Makes 7

It is not always easy to say for sure what we believe—about life in general or even about our personal Christian faith. As we grow older, some experiences leave us confused. We live with unanswered questions, ambiguities, paradoxes.

On the other hand, faith communities over the centuries—churches, denominations, parachurch organizations, Christian colleges—have traditionally formulated statements of faith as a way to affirm in words what their members believe. In some churches, people recite the Apostles' Creed or the Nicene Creed every Sunday, or on particular Sundays, as part of the liturgy. The Lord's Prayer often has a regular place in worship services. Some religious groups, like the Baptists or the Plymouth Brethren, have no creeds as such, but nonetheless they regard it as essential that all believers be able to "give an account of the faith that is in them" (paraphrase of 1 Peter 3:15).

As part of journal-keeping, it is important from time to time to try to clarify for yourself just where you now stand in your attitude toward life and faith. Therefore I suggest labeling the sixth notebook divider *Affirmations.*

For many years, at the start of each decade, one Christian magazine has run a multi-part series called "How My Mind Has Changed."[1] Prominent religious figures, often internationally known, are asked to write an article on that topic. Perhaps the origin in my mind of this idea for journal writing lies in my interest in that series.

In my New College journal workshops we begin the Sunday afternoon writing with two exercises in this category. I ask participants to take a clean sheet of notebook paper and head it with this title: "What I Used to Believe That I No Longer Believe." For this exercise I ask people simply to list some opinions they formerly held about matters of everyday life, as well as some of their past beliefs on "more spiritual" topics. (The second part of this writing exercise deals with present beliefs.) After each workshop I always wish I had a copy of everything the participants volunteered to read aloud in this category. This and its later companion exercise have elicited some of the most meaningful and poignant writing in my journal-keeping workshops.

Here are some responses I have received for inclusion in this book.

What I Used to Believe That I No Longer Believe

Lynn A: I used to believe that

- Everyone who went to church was a Christian.
- Faith in Christ somehow made it easy to overcome sin and temptation.
- I had to live up to the standards set by others for me.
- Singing and music-making were primarily the acquisition of technique and knowledge of rules.
- Having a good heart and feeling sorry for others was enough.
- "Wasting time" was frivolous and unnecessary.
- Relationships with people could fulfill all my relationship needs.

- Having a lot of friends was important.
- People would not love me if I was not perfect.

Pat: I used to believe that
- God was an angry god.
- I needed to earn his love.
- God could be worshiped only in silence and formality.
- God would love me more if I were thin.
- God's will for me was obscure and difficult to discern.

June: I used to believe that
- My mother was a blameless victim in the wreckage of my childhood.
- H. loved me.
- K. would always love me, and K. was very wise.
- I was ugly and probably stupid.
- I was clumsy.
- Breaking up with Y. would devastate me.
- I liked almost everybody.

Melissa: I used to believe that
- If you didn't go to church on Sunday, something terrible would happen.
- Someday there would be a "best friend" for me and we would agree on everything and have wonderful times together.
- If you saw it in print, it was true.
- Even if some kids lied, adults in responsible positions wouldn't.
- Hard work and accomplishments are always recognized and rewarded.
- A Christian husband would understand me fully, take care of me emotionally, and would always and truly be the spiritual leader of our family.
- If you did your best to be good parents, the kids would turn out pretty much as you hoped.

Jenny: I used to believe that

- There was no reason not to be scornful of others.
- If a school librarian recommended a book, I didn't want to read it.
- God had no real relevance in day-to-day life.
- It was important to prove oneself better than (superior to) others.
- (After becoming a Christian), Z. was the man of God's choice for me.

Mary: At age eight I believed that my soul looked like a big flat misshapen marshmallow that hung invisibly suspended between my neck and my waist. I believed that when I sinned "small sins," fuzzy grayish marks would appear on my soul. Bigger sins, the kind you went to hell for, caused black marks. After confession, the gray and black marks would disappear and for a very brief time the marshmallow would be perfectly white and clean.

"This is neither magic nor mechanical help—it is a spiritual skill."

After school on Fridays the nun would line us all up outside the confessional. As we waited for our turn in the little closet-like booth, we were supposed to think of all our sins. I was always ashamed to tell the priest what I had done, so I did the next best thing. I made up a list of fake sins and confessed those instead.

On Sundays we all went to communion. Again we were lined up to go up to the altar. There was no way out. I knew that if a person received communion while in a state of sin they were automatically excommunicated. I knew that meant me.

Those statements reflect "the way we were." Because our minds change, it helps to be clear about the ways in which they have changed. That takes us to the next journaling exercise, about our present outlook on both everyday matters and "more spiritual" concerns. The second part of the Affirmations exercise has this title: "What I Now Know to Be True about Life."

Lynn A: Now I know that

- It is important to share deeply with people (selectively).
- Only Christ can complete the fulfillment of my relationship needs; people can't.
- It is often most difficult to share deeply with those closest to me—i.e., parents, siblings, spouse.
- It is necessary to draw from my inner soul to convey the true meaning and emotion of meaningful music.
- I am not responsible for the success or failure of others around me.
- It is very hard always to be honest.
- Time does not equal money; money does not guarantee happiness.
- Guilt and bitterness are destructive.
- Beauty is not always perfect.

Pat: Now I know that

- Praying in tongues is a natural form of expression to my Father.
- God deepens my awareness and compassion.
- If I marry, it's because I can enhance the Kingdom that way.
- Loneliness is a given of human nature and is not exclusively the property of single adults.
- God has appointed to me a certain number of days, months, years, to serve him on earth.
- Nothing is forever except life in eternity.

June: Now I know that

- No one is entirely blameless or entirely culpable. My mother, and her marriages, helped create the situation of my childhood.

What I Now Know to Be True about Life

- Some people tell you they love you, but it doesn't necessarily mean anything.
- I have a tendency to create heroes.
- I am brighter than a great many people—not as bright as quite a few—and I am both more and less smart than I think I am. Intelligence has many facets, and doesn't guarantee common sense or integrity or, really, anything.
- I am not especially clumsy.
- Time heals. Traumas are seldom as bad as anticipated by one with an active imagination.
- Sex, compared to friendship, warmth, respect, is only a small part of life.
- I am often cranky, generally misanthropic (with notable exceptions).

Melissa: Now I know that
- One's background and early experience are tremendously influential on how you feel the rest of your life.
- Early parental attitudes are hard to separate from conscience and one's later personal outlook.
- Understanding the gospel has made a significant difference.
- A lot of Christians are truly people of good will, self-sacrifice, and generosity.
- A lot of Christians aren't that much different from those who profess no such faith—or in some cases are worse.
- It's hard not to say stupid things.
- Women are still judged largely by outward appearance.
- Unthinkable amounts of money go into vice.
- The best person doesn't always get the job.
- Good advice is hard to give and also hard to receive.

Jenny: Now I know that
- God cares for our kids and can get through to them in ways that we can't.

- Life has been, and is, good; amazing opportunities, "above all I could ask or think," have come to me.
- Color is a wonderful thing.
- God's timing is real and best.

Alice: Now I know that
- Life isn't always fair.
- Wanting something doesn't mean I'll get it.
- Aging is inevitable and irreversible.
- Spiritual growth usually comes through pain.
- God loves me unconditionally and forever.
- ONLY God loves me unconditionally and forever.
- The future will contain the unexpected.
- I will never be able to read all the books I want to read.
- The house will always get dirty again.

Lynn V: Now I know that
- God is good.
- In the midst of the joyous times he celebrates with me.
- In my dark moments he walks through the water with me and I won't drown.
- He sometimes gives me a panoramic view of my life and sometimes his lamp lights only my next step.
- I can trust him absolutely. He will never fail me.

Donnette: Now I know that
- Life changes continually.
- Patterns emerge through the ebb and flow of my days and seasons, yet they are always variations, not repetitions.
- Life is fragile—even at my strongest I am subject to fatigue, pain, and illness.
- Life is a gift from the hands of God, a gift he calls me to share with those around me.
- Life is a privilege and a responsibility.

- I am called to give my life back to God on a daily basis so that the hours of my day may be filled according to his will and purpose.
- The paths of God are mercy and truth. If I know the mercy of God, I need never fear the truth.

How has your mind changed? What did you once believe that you no longer believe? What do you now know to be true about life, about God?

The spiritual experience of Christians needs to be rooted in biblical concepts: God's love, his provision of forgiveness through Christ, his purpose for every human being—child or adult, male or female—independent of race, talents, or intellectual capabilities. This rootedness is a gradual, growing process.

But in this life we have only finite words to describe our experience of God. When we attempt to speak about God, as the above writers have done, we begin with the recognition that our human words are not fully adequate. Also, regrettably, we know that our spoken or written words, however well-intentioned and honestly articulated from our heart, may distort the divine reality for someone else who hears or reads them. Times change. Perspectives change. People's lives color what they hear and understand.

So when we write (and from time to time rewrite) our affirmations, when we attempt to give a "reason for the hope that is in us," we also recognize that it is the touch of the Spirit of God that makes a difference in people's lives, as it has in our own.

Note: When you have written these two exercises, file them under the sixth notebook divider, *Affirmations.*

Talking It Out

Journaling is not for people of unfaith . . . or for those who want to keep the status quo in their lives. It is for adventurers, for those who have a vision of another city, who hear the call given to Abraham to leave the old land and to set out for a new one.

Along the way you will have to do battle with the principalities of evil. The devil himself will try to shake your confidence. He will try to make you think you are not all that important—not really worth the effort.

Dis-ease shakes our confidence in what we can do, in who we are and in who we can become. We begin to doubt that there is a plan for us and a place where we fit in. Carried to its extreme, doubt whispers that God is not there and that he does not tend our life, that he will not complete what he has begun.

May the Lord, our God, keep us all persons of faith.

Elizabeth O'Connor
Letters to Scattered Pilgrims

Part 3

Writing When the Moment Spurs 8

Nothing encourages aspiring writers so much as to see in print something they have written. That's why the first assignment we give students in our New College writers' workshops is to compose (and send off) a "Letter to the Editor." It's necessary, of course, to mail any response to a newspaper story or article in a current magazine as soon as possible. (With the advent of FAX, speed is even more important if you're targeting a daily or weekly.) When students in the writers' workshop do that, they often are able to bring in a published letter to show to the rest of us before that five-week class ends.

Writing letters to the editor on topics of current interest is a way to break into print and to build up motivation for trying to do greater things. One contemporary novelist used a retired Catholic schoolteacher's response to a letter in an Irish periodical as a starting point for what he then developed into two novels in a series about small-town life in Minnesota.[1]

Another kind of letter is the response we pound out on the spur of the moment, in a hurry or in a fury, having built up a head of steam about something. Having written that letter, we don't always send it—especially if it's directed to someone we know firsthand, rather than merely to an unknown "faceless" editor.

The next journaling category, therefore (though usually not one I ask participants to write in during the weekend workshop), is actually a receptacle or depository. It comes under the seventh notebook divider, *Unsent Letters*. Here we have a safe place to unload and store our red-hot missives, or our missiles with fissionable potential, until they cool down or are de-nuked—before they start a chain reaction.

Can you remember writing a note or letter to someone, mailing it off, and almost immediately regretting it? Or have you ever written a note or letter, stashed it away for awhile, and then been glad you'd delayed sending it? As time passed, you realized that such a communique was probably better left in your own hands, unmailed. Several months after attending a journal workshop, a young woman told me she'd written a lot in this category to a certain male friend. Then one day she pulled out all those "unsent" letters and zapped them off to you-know-who. Not a good idea, unless you thrive on disaster.

Another faithful journal-keeper told me she wrote letters to her policeman husband, recently killed on the job, and also to her deceased parents. Then she took an out-of-state trip to the place where all of them were buried. Finding a lovely "bed and breakfast" nearby, she settled in for a week and eventually one beautiful morning went out to the cemetery. There she sat under a tree near their graves and read aloud those letters from her journal. She cried. She prayed. "A healing experience," she said. It brought her more peace than she had felt before. She had needed that closure. She knew that God was with her and would help her to live beyond tragedy and loneliness.

Thinking about these comments, I also recall one person I've looked up to for years, a long-time acquaintance to whom I once wrote two letters I eventually decided not to mail. The non-recipient was a prolific, nationally known personage, so her reputation was already intimidating to me. In the first instance she had just published an autobiography in which one chapter told about her participation in a "new age" study course that I knew had occult origins and was at its heart anti-Christian. Obviously many things that are not explicitly Christian can be helpful to a discerning person, but it concerned me that this writer's description of her experience in that "spiritually oriented" group was totally positive. Not even in a footnote in tiny six-point type had she acknowledged any potential problems, or cautioned naive readers to be careful about what they might be getting into.

I drafted my letter, responding as positively as I could to her autobiography as a whole but finally expressing my negative view of her unqualified enthusiasm for that study group. I reworked my letter many times but ended up not sending it. Was I a coward? Did I just not want to stir up trouble by being critical? Was I lazy, unwilling to put more time or energy into it? I'm not sure.

Several years later, a different issue arose with reference to this same person. Again I drafted a worried, questioning letter. Again I tried to be as affirming and diplomatic as possible. Again I did not mail it. Were both those issues worth raising? Yes, they were. Were my concerns justified? Again, yes.

But would I be heard? Would my attempt to spell out my reservations do any good, make a difference? Could I somehow influence her by expressing my concerns? Probably not, I thought. "Everyone's adrenocortico-steroids are limited," my biochemist husband commented laconically, so I should be careful about how I expend my dwindling allotment.

"When I see my thoughts on paper, translated to a page, they get cut down to size."

As a result, drafts of those two letters, heavily edited, remain among my "unsent letters." I'm glad I've kept them. They give me insight into myself: by nature (or by training) I am a reformer. Rereading those letters, I see what kinds of concerns have stirred me to scribal passion if not to outward action. They are evidence that I cared, even if my insecurity or cowardice or abject "desire to be liked" by someone smart and important prevented my actually mailing them. Perhaps category seven in my journal is the best place for those letters after all.

In *The New Diary,* Tristine Rainer devotes five pages to discussing unsent letters as a journaling technique. It's a way to ease your mind, she says, and then get on with your life. It can be a step toward resolution of an issue or a problematic relationship. It is also a tool toward "self-definition, since who you are is partly defined by whom you reach out to and include as audience in your inner life."[2] That includes my acquaintance-friend above.

After attending a New College journal workshop, *Lorna* decided to write a letter to her father.

Dear Dad,

When you turned 71 last Sunday, it hit me that one of these years I'll have to give you up. Grandpa lived only nine years beyond the age you are now.

Sometimes I wish I could drop in and tell you what's happening in my life and ask you how the livestock markets are at home. You kept me up to date on that all through my college years—I loved the way you always wrote and asked if my roommate and I thought you should sell the cattle for a certain price, as if it mattered what we thought. But it mattered that you asked anyway. My friends were always amazed that my dad wrote so many letters.

I guess I'll always have a special feeling about those times before breakfast when I could ride with you on the tractor if I got up to help you do early morning chores. Somehow you managed to make each one of us feel important. I just want you to know that I still remember.

Love,
Lorna

Women, Rainer continues, have a tendency to "think in writing," especially to men.[3] In their diaries or journals they put down thoughts and feelings they would never be able to say in person, as well as sometimes writing letters they would never dare to send. Thus, the unsent letter can be a catharsis, as Aristotle noted long ago about the effect of dramatic tragedy on theater audiences. Writing can be a helpful way to relieve tension, spell it out, sound off. As a result, we know what we think. It is clear where we stand. Life can go on. And we haven't "made things worse" or hurt someone else in the process.

Another "unsent letter" was written by *Sandy* to a former college friend, Bob:

Dear Bob:

Seeing the twenty-year reunion picture of our class in the alumni magazine today, I got to thinking about you. For whatever reason, neither of us made it back there. Twenty years is a long time to have been out of touch with someone I once liked, so maybe this anniversary of our graduation makes it appropriate to write.

I wonder if you ever think of the times we dated and were close (in terms of the Christian mores of that era), the long talks we had every day before and after classes, meeting each other's parents, etc. Surely you knew I cared about you, and I thought, for awhile, that I was special to you too. But how could you take me to the airport before Christmas, say you'd see me "next year," and then never call me?

Your best friend, Matt, told me he'd often told you he thought I was "the woman for you," so I knew I was being discussed by the two of you in those terms. Matt wouldn't have said that to me if your response had been "Never! Not on your life!" Rather, it made me hopeful. Our relationship those days seemed like a portent of joy ahead, in contrast with my experience of men (boys) in the past. It took me years to recover from the crisis of faith that overwhelmed me when it became undeniable that you had moved out of my life forever. I remember your once quoting something you'd learned years before in Bible school: "Disappointments? *His* appointments."

I repeated that disarming incantation to myself again and again, trying to believe it and acquiesce in God's will. But now I think it reflected a kind of hyper-Calvinism, perhaps beyond your own beliefs, that for me was more destructive than helpful. It made it hard to keep on trusting God.

Now I think, instead, that my disappointment was not God's appointment; it was not what he would have chosen had his will been determinant. I think God was grieved when you checked out on me like that. You were of course a product of a sexist society in which males clearly had the right to choose and to reject, to call or not to call—and no questions could be raised by the woman (girl) involved.

So much in this world is *not* the way God wants it. How much better it is to have confidence that God suffers when we do, feels our personal pain just as intensely, feels the world's anguish—and longs for things to be otherwise. To believe *that* seems wiser than to think that God disapproved of my love for you, and then left me desolate and confused.

To be a woman in this culture, in most cultures, is often a paradoxical, powerless, and frustrating state of being. I cannot believe that God approves of half his human creation being hurt in the ways girls and women so often get hurt. I am not blaming you. Well, maybe I am, for not being more kind-hearted in your greater spiritual maturity, for using your "male prerogative of choice" in a situation that only a little imagination would have told you needed careful handling.

I have been married to a remarkable man for sixteen years, and because I know him to be God's choice for me I don't look back and think "it might have been." But I wonder if there is healing for this breach that now has spanned two decades. If you and your wife and family are ever in our part of the country, I hope you will look us up. Wouldn't you like to know what a strong and different woman I have become? I do not look on myself as only a helpmeet or appendage to my husband's call-ing. I am egalitarian in outlook, as is he.

I am glad that I didn't lose my Christian faith over you. Rather, recognizing my human fallenness, selfishness, inad-equacy, and powerlessness, I continued to believe that the out-reach of God to me, through his Word, through Jesus, had to be "good news." Now, I love a lot of people—and sometimes I know I am loved by them as well. I have given up some of my fears, one evidence of that being my writing this "unsent letter."

I recall that, whatever the weather, you used to jog six miles a day; I've run three and a half at best, but mostly two. A lot of thoughts come to mind, and might be freely expressed, while circling the track with a one-time friend.

Sandy

(Sandy did decide to write to Bob—not this letter but a shorter, less explicit one. He replied very soon, perhaps with his wife looking over his shoulder, saying he didn't know he had been all that important to her.)

"The human encounter is difficult," someone has observed, "because it leads to that wounding experience, . . . the exhaus-tion of the only-human."[4]

A situation somewhat similar to Sandy's, told from a male point of view, had a more noble outcome. In an article in *Faith at Work* magazine, editor Walden Howard described once writing a "dialogue" with a girlfriend from his distant past. Because she, like Sandy, was someone he had "walked away from" without explanation or apology, he realized he still had "unfinished business" with her that he needed to take care of. Although it wasn't easy to locate her so many years later, he finally discovered her address in a city two thousand miles away. Later, when he was in that city on a trip, he vis-ited her and apologized for his thoughtless behavior forty years before. Then, he writes, "we shared our journeys over the intervening years, and I went away feeling 'finished' about the transaction."[5]

That reconciliation, Howard explained, arose from his participation in an "Intensive Journal" workshop sponsored by Dialogue House. "If I were to pursue only one discipline for personal growth other than daily Bible reading and prayer," he wrote in that same article, "I would choose to keep an 'intensive journal.'"[6]

Note: At least for the time being, file your spur-of-the-moment epistles under the seventh notebook divider, *Unsent Letters.*

Journal Conversations 9

Letters are the voice of one person speaking to another, or sometimes to several persons. So are monologues and lectures. But a conversation moves back and forth.

In her book on diaries, Tristine Rainer noted that psychoanalyst Carl G. Jung (1875–1961) frequently wrote "imaginary conversations" in his journals as a means of self-study. Then, "in the 1960s, Gestalt therapists began using the technique of the imaginary dialogue to help people become aware of various aspects of their personalities." A hundred years before that, however, novelist George Sand (a woman who took a male pen name) had also written "imaginary inner dialogues in her diary."[1]

The contemporary writing out of such dialogues is an idea now made famous by Ira Progoff, who in the mid-1960s turned the highly structured journal-keeping format he had created into a business under the name of Dialogue House. Today, many journal-keeping courses and workshops reflect the influence of Progoff's "Intensive Journal" program.

It is a small step from the unsent letters of chapter 8 in this book to writing out imaginary conversations with persons important in your life. One factor necessary to producing a "paper conversation" or "journal conversation" is that you care about your relationship with the person with whom you choose to "converse"—and believe that the relationship needs to go somewhere. Another prerequisite is that you have a fairly good sense of what is significant to the person you now try to "talk with" on paper; you are aware to some extent of how that person's life has gone. If you can list a few of his or her "turning points," that will help.

So, divider number eight in your journal notebook can be labeled *Conversations.* Eventually it may have a number of subdivisions, as you repeat this exercise with various persons important to you. Take a clean sheet of paper and title it "Conversation with (Dick)" or "Conversation with (Jane)." After trying to note some of Dick or Jane's turning points, write a brief factual statement, no more than a couple of sentences, about what the situation is between the two of you right now.

Although an argument may develop in the course of your back-and-forth interaction, the object of writing a journal conversation is not primarily to argue or to settle any differences between you. Your differences may come to light, but you need to begin addressing the other person in a pleasant, friendly manner and then see what happens. You speak first, but don't start with a question. Then, what does the person say in response? What do you say next? Keep going, even if it sounds like a record you've played a hundred times. If you get stuck, admit it. Write, "Look, I'm drawing a blank. I don't know what to say next." Then what does the other person reply?

Writing a journal conversation is like writing a play.

Me:

Dick (or Jane):

Me:

Dick (or Jane):

(And so on.)

Go into this written discussion open-endedly, just to encounter the other person. It might be a friend, parent, sibling, spouse, son, daughter, other relative. It might be a coworker or your boss. Here are two examples.

Journal conversation between *Sue* and her husband, Dennis:

Factual Statement: Dennis and I have been married for over three years. Currently I am frustrated that we don't talk enough and that it's hard to get answers and responses from him. I would like to have him initiate some times together, even regular ones, rather than always turning to the TV for company.

Sue: Hi, honey. You look tired. Would you like to come and sit for a while?

Dennis: I don't know, I guess that's okay.

Sue: What are you feeling or thinking?

Dennis: Tired.

Sue: That's a physical feeling. What about emotions?

Dennis: I don't know. I guess I don't want to do anything for a while. Maybe sleep or watch TV.

Sue: Oh.

(Silence for a minute or two)

Sue: Is there a better time to talk with you, when you'll be more alert and able to share?

Dennis: I guess. Sometime later.

Sue: Could we set a time so that I'll know I'll get a chance to say things and have your attention and vice versa? I really need to have a time to talk with you about what's happening in my life: my feelings and thoughts and ideas. Do you ever have a need to do that?

Dennis: I guess I just do it all inside. The times I try to tell you about what interests me, like the news or science or my job, you don't seem interested.

Sue: I think that when it comes to the news or anything controversial, I'm afraid it'll get all involved and we'll disagree or argue and I don't like that. I don't feel comfortable with conflict between us, even if it's not really serious. I guess I feel threatened, or that you won't like me—or maybe *I* won't like me. So, I just avoid those conversations.

Dennis: It's okay not to agree with me. Then we can see why we disagree. Who knows, maybe we'll agree on a lot of things.

Sue: I suppose, but it's still hard, and it still seems less personal. It's not *your* thoughts and reactions and feelings about what's happening to *you*, but it's with other people, strangers. I'm more interested in what's going on inside of *you*.

Dennis: I'm not sure I see the difference. Those are my thoughts, so they are part of what's inside me.

Sue: But it's not the same. It's not generated out of your own experiences. Or maybe it's the emotional part that I sense is missing. That's the part I connect to.

Dennis: I think the feelings are harder for me to identify and to verbalize.

Sue: I know. I'd be glad to help you, but I need your permission and openings.

Journal conversation between *Walt* and his daughter, Christine, an interpreter for the deaf:

Factual Statement: Christine, age 27, is living on her own, is on good terms with us, but is not always open about what's going on.

Dad: Hi, Little Sweetheart. This is your used-uppie old Dad talking to your yuppie-type answering machine. How about giving us a call?

Christine: (clicking off machine) How about talking to you right now?

Dad: Hey, I found your actual person in person.

Christine: Yep, it's me, all right.

Dad: (in artificial speech) Hello - Christine. This - is - your - father's - machine - talking - to - you. I - got - lonely - and - so - I - called - up - your - answering - machine. I - thought - I - would - whisper - sweet - nothings - in - its - receiver. But - if - you - have - turned - it - off - I - will - put - your - father - back - on - the - phone. Here - he - is.

Christine: Oh, Dad, I love you.

Dad: I love you, too! How're you doing?

Christine: Oh, pretty good. Still haven't put a dent in my new car.

Dad: Just a big dent in your finances, I guess.

Christine: Oh, yeah, but let's not talk about that. I don't think about it much. At least not all the time.

Dad: Well, you've got maybe six months before the crunch comes. Do you think there's no chance your job will get funded?

Christine: No, I'll have to find something else, but I'm not going to worry about that now.

Dad: Any ideas?

Christine: Oh, yeah. With a car I can do a lot of interpreting jobs I couldn't have done before.

Dad: Can you find enough work that way to support you?

Christine: I don't know. But I said I'm not going to worry about that now. You shouldn't worry about it either.

Dad: Well, there's a lot of difference between worrying and thinking.

Christine: I know, and I'm thinking about it.

Dad: And praying? I guess if I had your kind of payments to make I'd be doing a lot of praying.

Christine: Don't you pray a lot anyway?

Dad: Sure. One reason our house payments are low is that it was falling apart when we bought it. I pray that the Lord will hold it together 'til I can do something about it. Great spiritual exercise. Same with our old VWs. I keep praying that at least one of 'em will start when we need 'em.

Christine: Well, you can always roll it down the hill to start it.

Dad: Right. I can see why you had to buy a *new* car. You live in the flatlands. Makes sense.

Christine: Oh, Dad, you're so funny. Actually I do worry about it, a lot.

Dad: Well, you had to have a car. If you belong to God, he knows you need transportation, so he probably helped you pick that one out.

Christine: I hope so. I'm afraid I just bought the one I wanted.

Dad: Well, he knows how you operate. He probably took that into account. I mean, you could have fallen in love with a Cadillac.

Christine: Oh, Dad, I love you. I hope you're not disappointed in me.

Dad: Disappointed? No, sweetheart. I just want what's best for you. And I want you to stay financially solvent—so you can support me in my old age.

Christine: Dad, you're never going to get old.

Dad: Well, I'm not worrying about it, but I'm thinking.

Christine: That's good. You know there's a big difference between thinking and worrying.

Dad: I'm glad I called. You're always full of good advice.

Christine: Any time, Dad.

These journal conversations reflect the way each writer thought they *might* go. A second approach is to write the conversation the way you *hope* it will go. Usually there's a difference, and that difference is worth reflecting on.

Some relationships are so important, or so complicated, that you may need to write several conversations with a particular person in order to reach a level that satisfies you or that leads to a breakthrough. But if that doesn't happen, and if you have written realistically, at least you will have a fairly accurate portrayal of what you sense your relationship with that person is like.

You can also write this kind of conversation with someone important to you who is no longer living. The fact that a person is dead doesn't mean they no longer impact your life. In my workshops, choosing to write an imaginary back-and-forth with a dead parent has often turned into a remarkable experience for the writer.

In a letter after the workshop, *Karen* wrote:

[Writing the journal conversation] got me in touch with my feelings about my dead father. I had had some very upsetting feelings about him: the fact that he died suddenly while I was in Guatemala, that I didn't even find out until a week later, that we never had a very good farewell; all that troubled me. Doing the writing, I got an overwhelming sense of the love we had for each other that was so powerful it made me cry (not an easy thing for me). I received, for the first time, a sense that our love made all the things that weren't right all right. That was a very beautiful thing for me to experience, and I wanted to tell you about it. The odd thing is that the writing doesn't read like anything very special now, even to me.

Nancy's experience was similar to Karen's:

I wrote a conversation with my dad who died when I was six (thirty-seven years ago!). He was an M.D. and at age thirty-seven had great dreams and plans of doing medical work in Afghanistan, a country closed to regular Christian missionaries. (I've heard that Mom and Dad had spread maps in the living room to plan strategy.) Well, he was young and still full of hope and faith, but he died suddenly, overnight, of a heart attack in the middle of it all. It took me over thirty years to begin to grieve in any deep way, consciously I mean.

In the past several years I've done some processing of it, but writing this conversation has been something new, in three major areas. First and most important, it resolved for me somewhat the untimeliness of Daddy's death. Nothing will take away from the tragedy of that, but I realized in this writing what a gift it was to me that I got to have him at his best.

Second, this is the first time I've articulated the connection between his absence and my questions about God, and more, about church.

Third, it has opened the door to a new level of passion associated with spiritual reality in particular and with life in general. I note the lack of passion in what I wrote (is this because I was six and sort of pre-sexual?) Is it because he lacked some passion in his compulsivity? Seeing my own compulsivity—I noted how I stepped out of intimacy in the writing to proceed with the "assignment"—gave me hope that I have more power than I thought, to effect change in my relationships. I have longed for greater intimacy, and maybe there are some things I can do to facilitate that.

So I guess what happened is that I can love what I had with Daddy, realize it is very idealized, and let it be just that: an ideal to pull me on, and not a curse by which to measure myself, my husband (that's been the worst of it), and others (including the church). "Them's no small potatoes in my book," and it was the journal conversation that catalyzed it.

Why go to all the effort of writing out these paper conversations in your journal? For several reasons. First, it's a way to allow yourself to get beneath the surface of everyday matters. Second, it's a safe way to try out new directions in relating to the other person and sense where those directions might lead. Third, by rereading what you have written, you often can find out what you want (or wanted) from this relationship. Here is one more example:

Journal conversation between *Donnette* and Judy:

Factual Statement: Judy, I'm not sure of your turning points, but I know you were born a twin; you were an Army nurse in Vietnam, an alcoholic, recovering in AA, lost within yourself, a suicide.

Donnette: I'm sorry I was the last person to talk to you before you killed yourself.

Judy: You always were good at feeling guilty, weren't you?

Donnette: You reached out to many of your friends in your last days and hours. Why didn't you listen to us?

Judy: I wanted to make you all sorry for not being what I wanted you to be.

Donnette: We tried, Judy, but we couldn't. You were too demanding.

Judy: I deserved more. I suffered a lot, gave a lot. It was time for others to take care of me.

Donnette: God calls us to serve, to pour ourselves out into the lives of others. Why did you lie to me when I called? I wanted to meet for coffee and talk and listen. You used to say I was the only person with whom you could be totally honest, but the last thing you said to me was a lie.

Judy: I had already decided to die. You couldn't have stopped me.

Donnette: There was an article in the paper about you last week. You would have been pleased with all the attention. I'm angry at you because of the guilt I feel. The last time I saw you I was impatient with you. I thought you were being petulant and childish. Your drunkenness disgusted and frightened me. I knew you were capable of violence. I'm sorry I was rude and impatient.

Judy: I was so lost in myself that it didn't matter. I couldn't hear through the haze of booze and pills. I wanted you to tell me that everything would be all right, that I would someday marry and be happy, be taken care of.

Donnette: I couldn't, Judy. There are no guarantees in life. You knew that the Lord could help you, but you weren't willing to pay the price. You knew that healing comes through surrender, commitment, trust, faith in God, and willingness to accept his will. But you couldn't stop trying to force your will on God, make him play by your rules.

Judy: That's not true. I trusted God, but he wasn't enough.

Donnette: Oh, Judy, you wouldn't let him be. I release you to his care and wish you peace. Goodbye, dear Judy. I loved you, my friend.

Note: File your paper conversation with Dick or Jane under the eighth notebook divider, *Conversations.* As you go on to write such journal conversations with various people, it helps to add subsections to this category, using a different kind of notebook divider for each person's name.

Just As I Am 10

For some people, journal-keeping is a preamble to Christian faith. It facilitates and in time can lead to their commitment to the God of Abraham, Isaac, and Jacob, the God of Miriam, Deborah, and Huldah.[1] In a 1976 doctoral dissertation, a man who had once been a student of Ira Progoff documented his own experience in using "intensive journal" methods to help people "deepen and grow in their inward spiritual life . . . [it was] a means of Christian nurture."[2]

Evaluations from my workshops, too, invariably reflect the participants' realization that keeping a journal will benefit them spiritually. Although different people respond to different journal-writing exercises, by far the most positive response has been to another approach to conversational writing. Divider number nine in your journal notebook can be given the title, *Conversations with God (or Jesus)*.

Writing a conversation with God or Jesus (or for that matter, with the Holy Spirit) may seem shocking at first. But it is also reminiscent of what has been described as "conversational prayer"—that is, talking to God in your own words, being as natural and honest and open about your life as possible. As in the journal conversation with a human person (chapter 9), here you try to write what you imagine would be the "response." At its most basic level, of course, this exercise will show you what your perception of the divine person really is.

That perception is revealed in what you "hear" being said back to you. Are you ready to try?

But, you may ask, is what I write as the "reply" actually divinely inspired? Maybe. Maybe not. Does it reflect—is it congruent with—the loving God, the loving Savior, seen in Scripture? Rereading what you have written, you must always ask yourself that question.

A small book by Cheryl Biehl called *Scriptural Meditation* is subtitled "The Listening Side of Prayer." In it she describes her personal experience in writing conversations with God, addressing him directly in her journal. She begins by reading and then responding to a verse or a short passage from the Bible. First, she says,

1. I pray and ask God to fill my mind completely with *His* thoughts.
2. I ask Him to guard my mind against thoughts from the enemy.
3. Then I read and write out the phrase or verse on which I will meditate, and I begin to write my thoughts.

"For me, journal-keeping is like obeying the scriptural admonition to the Israelites that they 'not tear down the landmarks.' It helps me remember who I am."

Cheryl then records in her journal what she believes are the words of God or of Jesus speaking to her in reply.[3]

The present "journal conversation" I am proposing is something like that. The format is the same as in the earlier exercise.

Me:

God (or Jesus):

Me:

God (or Jesus):

Certainly we don't want to put our own words in God's mouth, nor do we want to be self-deceived. So, after taking a few minutes to be quiet and perhaps to pray, you might begin writing this dialogue by expressing such a concern. I did just that when I was introduced to an exercise something like this, but with a different title.[4] In the very first journal workshop I attended, one not explicitly Christian, my "paper conversation" went like this:

Ginny's Conversation with God:

Me: You know how tired I am, but I'm used to talking with you and being open. So maybe I'm up to trying that.

God: I'm listening. I always am.

Me: Yes. But I don't want to pick up on a voice of my own psyche and mistake it for yours.

God: If you do, I can get through that. I have a lot of ways to get to you.

Me: Yes, some surprising ones. I see that today—how you still get through to people individually, when the conventional forms are no longer effective—or even repel them. [And so on.]

Louise also began her "paper conversation" a bit apprehensively and found herself taking a "safe" approach by quoting verses she recalled from the Bible.

Me: Father, this is difficult for me to start; it seems presumptive even to assume that we can talk back and forth. I have trouble imagining it. It seems too sacred, and I feel unworthy.

God: If with all your heart you truly seek me, you shall ever surely find me.

Me: Sometimes you seem very far away, and I despair.

God: I have loved you with an everlasting love; therefore with lovingkindness have I drawn you.

Me: I know that you want me to come, and that Jesus died to make my coming to you possible.

God: Yes, I provided the Way. [And so on.]

Lynne, too, began cautiously:

Me: I'm afraid of this "conversation," Lord.

Lord: Why is that? Are you afraid of Me?

Me: Not really—well, yes. Mostly I'm afraid I'll try to put words in your mouth, and sometimes I'm afraid of what you might ask of me.

Lord: Have I ever asked you to do something and not helped you do it?

Me: No, but sometimes it has hurt.

Lord: Do you remember the hurt more—or the peace?

Me: The peace.

Lord: Then, why are you still afraid? I want you to grow, so sometimes I have to tear down the walls you have built up and haul away the trash. [And so on.]

During the nineteenth century an Anglican woman named Charlotte Elliott wrote hundreds, perhaps thousands, of poems addressing God directly and letting him know her daily concerns. Although some of her poems have titles like "A Song in the Night," "Thoughts on a Birthday," "The Wild Violet," "A Winter Sunset," "My Home," "Summer Evening by the Seaside," "On a Spring Morning," and "For a Sunday in Solitude," many of them are really prayers. Writing poetry was her way of conversing with God.[5]

One of Charlotte Elliott's poems is still widely known as a hymn. She titled it "Just As I Am." Christians as disparate in their emphases as evangelist Billy Graham and Harvard professor Harvey Cox have written about the influence of that hymn on their lives as young men. Listen to the "testimony" of Cox in his autobiography:

For me [the words of that hymn] still convey a sense of comfort and assurance. Was I really acceptable to God "just as I am"? Was it really true that I needed no improvements, no alterations, that I could enter the presence of the Most High, the terrifying *mysterium tremendum* (as I later learned to say) *just* as I am? If true, that was very good news to an adolescent who was always being reminded—or so it seemed to me—of my shortcomings and defects. I was never good at football or basketball. Someone else played the saxophone sweeter than I did. Most of the girls seemed to prefer other guys for dates. Although I did fairly well in my classes there was always someone, usually one of the girls, who got a higher score on the exam. Both my parents seemed to love me unconditionally but, like all kids, I sensed behind their expressions of affection a lot of hopes and expectations I was not sure I could live up to.

But God accepted me just as I am?

That was not judgment but good news.[6]

The phrase, "just as I am," describes the spirit in which to write this next "journal conversation." "Just as I am" is also the mind-set that should characterize all our journal-keeping. There is no point in trying to kid God or misrepresent ourselves in any way.

The Book of Psalms has many examples of writers pouring out their heart to God. In my workshops I begin the Sunday afternoon session by reading part of Psalm 139, which I think is particularly apt as a "journal-keeper's psalm":

O Lord, you know everything about me . . .
You know my every thought . . .
I can never be lost to your Spirit!
I can never get away from my God!

verses 1, 2, 7 LB, adapted

When you try to write this extraordinary dialogue, you can forthrightly acknowledge whatever is currently on your mind. As with the conversation in chapter 9, it helps if you begin with a brief factual statement.

This was *Nancy's*:

Factual Statement: Everybody else says they know what God thinks about doctrine. They all seem to know the original Greek, but they all disagree. I'd like to hear it from God himself.

Me: Jesus, there is just so much I'm confused about.

Jesus: What is it? Tell me about it.

Me: Well, first of all, I have all these questions about who has the right doctrine.

Jesus: Oh, you too? Well, let's see. What have we got to choose from? There's Baptist, Methodist, Presbyterian . . .

Me: Excuse me, but I was thinking more along the lines of Calvinist vs. Arminian, Pentecostal vs. anti-Pentecostal, dispensationalist, amillennialist . . .

Jesus: Oh, I see. What troubles you about them?

Me: (thinking it quite obvious) They all disagree.

Jesus: They disagree. And that bothers you?

Me: Yes!

Jesus: (matter of factly) You want to know who's right. Why is that so important?

Me: So I can be right! So I'll know the right answer!

Jesus: Is there an exam coming up?

Me: No, of course not. Well, yes. Maybe. I just want to know. I want to be right!

Jesus: Okay. Let's see, what is it the Calvinists believe again? Predestination, right?

Me: (whining) Lo-ord!

Jesus: And some of them sprinkle babies and they may be amillennial, and some definitely do not believe in tongues. Anything I left out? Now the Arminians, on the other hand . . .

Me: (crossly) I don't think you're taking this very seriously.

Jesus: Was it something I said?

Me: You're making fun of it! I'm serious. These are important issues.

Jesus: (surprised) They are?

Me: (impatient) Of course!

Jesus: Why?

Me: I told you. I need to know who's right, who has the correct answers, the inside story, the best formula.

Jesus: Why is that?

Me: (angry) So you'll like me better!

Jesus: What?

Me: (quieter) So you'll like me better. I'll be a better person, and you'll like me better . . . Won't you?

Jesus: No.

Me: You won't?

Jesus: Nancy, I couldn't possibly love you more than I do right now.

Me: You couldn't?

Jesus: You say you want the best formula, the right answer, to attain more of God's love? Nancy, look at the cross. My blood was shed for you. Were you perfect on the day when they nailed me to the cross?

Bertha's Conversation with God:

Me: I have many fears in my life right now. The sight in my left eye isn't good. Some situations at work are scary, and I'm afraid of failing.

God: Remember when you were twenty-one and afraid to stay by yourself? I spoke to you through my Word, assuring you that I was with you.

Me: I remember. I really messed things up in those years. When I was eighteen I thought I knew all the answers and I got married when I was so poorly prepared for it. That marriage was destined to break up, and then I was alone with a son to raise.

God: Remember, I brought you into a small church fellowship that became your family. I let you live close to your sister and brother-in-law, and they treated you well.

Me: I had to work awfully hard to provide for myself and my son those nine years.

God: Remember? I made it possible for you to get vocational nurse's training; and to be an LVN was something you had wanted since you were five years old. I knew that you liked taking care of the sick.

Me: Well, it meant that my son had to stay by himself a lot.

God: I gave him good health. He was in sports, and that helped keep him busy. I put you in a small town, where other people knew him and watched over him. I sent my angels to care for him.

Me: Yes, but I had to wait until I was thirty-two to find another husband.

God: Now just stop a minute and listen to me. *I* provided a special person for you, a man who had a heart for me. Remember how patient he was with your son, and claimed him as his own. Hollis has been my gift to you.

Me: I had to have a hysterectomy; it took its toll on me.

God: I did pull you through, though, and in the meantime I gave you three more children. You forget so quickly.

Me: Six years after that, I got breast cancer and had to have a mastectomy.

God: That was seven years ago and you're still there on earth. Who is responsible for that: your doctor or me?

Me: Okay, Lord. I get the message. I will trust you with my life. And I'll be brave at work when I need to go into those scary situations.

In writing their paper conversations, two other persons also expressed concerns about marriage and the struggles they were facing.

Margaret's Conversation with Jesus:

Factual Statement: Jesus is my Lord and Savior, whom I've believed in intellectually as the Son of God for nine or ten years, but whom I really met personally only a little over three years ago. He is now my friend and the One I often pray to.

Me: Lord, I'm confused. I believe you want to save Nick. I believe he wants to be saved. Yet the process seems to be hitting so many snags. Is that necessary?

Jesus: Was it all smooth sailing for you?

Me: Well, it seems like it was. It seems like once you started drawing me toward you, my spiritual growth was pretty steady.

Jesus: Do you think it looked steady to me?

Me: I guess not. Was I really such a slow learner?

Jesus: You were. You all are. I have to wait for your surrenders, and they're never as big a surrender as you think. You all hand over your lives very reluctantly, bit by bit.

Me: But can't you speed up the process? After all, isn't faith really a gift from you? I know you've given me that gift in great abundance, with beautiful joy and support from Christian friends, all undeserved by me. Nick's been struggling longer than I ever did, and he needs to know you. Why can't you help him along faster? Doesn't he just get more stuck in his rut, the longer you leave him on his own?

Jesus: I haven't left him on his own. Haven't you noticed the ways I reach out to him, through TV programs, through magazine articles, even through you? Can't you see me carrying him forward?

Me: But Lord, won't it take more than that? I don't count, because I have to love him. I'm his wife. Couldn't you send him a Christian friend? He wants so much to feel he's loved, that he belongs. Why can't you find him the right group, the right friend?

Jesus: Quit telling me my business. Didn't I know how to woo you? And a difficult case you were too! Did you ever think you're supposed to be a channel of my love to Nick? What do you ever do to make him feel he belongs, to draw him into your Christian life?

Me: But Lord, I don't want to preach at him. That's not a wife's place.

Jesus: Not preach. Open up. Let him see into your life with me. I've given you such joy now, in work and friends, such growth and new insight. You always share those things with your Christian friends. You draw *them* into the joy I give you. Why not do that with Nick?

Me: Lord, I just can't talk to him. He's so unresponsive, I can't tell what he thinks. And he used to make such fun of my faith. It hurt.

Jesus: Has he made fun of you, or of your Christian friends, lately?

Me: No, not really.

Jesus: Then how about beginning to draw him into the circle?

Me: Wouldn't a small group be better?

Jesus: Maybe *you're* the best small group for him right now. You're great in small groups. Be a little more giving to the husband I've given you.

Me: It'll be hard breaking out of old patterns.

Jesus: I specialize in that. I know it may be uncomfortable. Do you love Nick enough to risk the awkwardness, the discomfort?

Me: I don't know. Are you sure you want me to talk more openly with him?

Jesus: Haven't I been waiting years already for you to do that? You're dense, Margie, but I've hung in there with you. Just like I'm hanging in there with Nick. You'll see.

Carol's Conversation with God:

Me: Are you there, God? It's me, Carol.

God: I am always here, Carol.

Me: Next month will mark the tenth anniversary of Mell's death.

God: Time has a way of slipping away.

Me: I thought by now I would have forgotten much of our life together and put my attention on other things. Why after all this time does it hurt so much to think of him and what we would be doing were he still here with us?

God: Because your heart is soft, and you had a good life. You may never forget.

Me: I guess I don't really want to forget; I just would like there to be room in my heart for someone else. It's as if he's the only soulmate or spiritual lover I can have, and that scares me. I will soon be fifty and I don't want to grow old alone. He would have been so much fun to grow old with—he loved life and us and you so much. What if I don't ever find anyone else to love like that?

God: Are you looking for someone else like that?

Me: I thought I had found that person in Larry. For years I waited patiently while he struggled with my loving him because he didn't understand how I could love him while he "chased skirts" and partied. I was so sure that, when he came around, our lives would be perfect.

Now he has decided he loves me and wants to spend the rest of his life with me. But I have decided he can't fulfill the needs I have now, especially the emotional and spiritual ones. So I prefer to remain lovers and friends, no more. This isn't what I had planned at all. I am upset, discouraged, confused, and nervous at the prospect of starting over again, just as if we were divorcing after eight years together.

God: What about the children?

Me: They are the reason I feel so upset. For the first couple of years with Larry I neglected them in ways I cannot even face right now; somehow I must confront each of them and beg their forgiveness. And though I know that was not Larry's fault, I think I blame him for that neglect while I pursued him, licking my wounds of widowhood. They know that his background is very different and that he is not a Christian; as a matter of fact, I can't even say they like him.

God: Do you like him?

"In my journal I am able to sort through some major stresses in my life and find God meeting me in them."

Me: (long pause) I must like him. I thought I loved him. He says he loves me. But I don't respect him because he doesn't respect himself; it all seems to come back to his alley cat morals and values. When I write these things they sound so much worse than they felt when I just thought them.

God: Is he good to you and for you?

Me: (long pause) Tracy asked me that recently, except she asked if he made me a better person. Remembering that, I hang my head and answer, "No."

God: Sounds as if this needs more attention.

Me: I know it does, and I'm afraid to look any deeper because I know that the answers will reveal some weakness in me for staying with this relationship for eight years. Please hang on, God. This may be rough on me.

God: I am always here, Carol.

Note: File the conversations you write in this category under the ninth notebook divider, *Conversations with God (or Jesus)*.

Afterwords

Part 4

It is often impossible for partly conscious, educated modern men and women to bring the totality of themselves before God without using a journal. . . .

Morton Kelsey
*Adventure Inward: Christian Growth
through Personal Journal Writing*

[Two myths] tend to inhibit journal writing. One is the perception of life as static instead of dynamic. The other is the denial of introspection as a meaningful function in our society. . . . I end up seeing myself at age seventy sitting in an overstuffed chair with volumes and volumes of journals piled around my feet. And I will be smiling at all that is tucked away on paper, not because it is brilliant, but because its mundaneness communicates my very human experience and my individuality.

Christina Baldwin
*One to One: Self-Understanding
through Journal Writing*

How It Started for Me 11

Being cut off from a part of one's story is apt to veil it in the haze of nostalgia, which is an ineffectual relationship to the past, and the haze of alienation, which is an ineffectual relationship to the present . . . I fall into the kind of musing that comes upon one in the netherspace of airplanes. . . . The country of my childhood lives within me with a primacy that is a form of love.[1]

Participants in my journal-keeping workshops sometimes ask how I got started in journaling. This is my story.[2]

When I was eight years old and in third grade, I was given a shiny red diary for Christmas by a family friend. One week later, on January 1, I made my first entry: "We went to the show."

After that, my occasional notations (in handwriting so bad I can hardly believe it was mine—we had just learned to write longhand that year) were likewise unimaginative. They do reflect a little of what life was like for a grade-school child in the small southern Wisconsin town in which I grew up.

There were music lessons, sibling spats and quarrels, spell-downs at school, valentines, May baskets, autograph books, movie-star pictures on the back of Dixie cup lids, five-cent ice cream cones, church programs for Children's Day and Christmas, friends coming over to play after school, trips to the library, visits to relatives for Sunday dinners, birthdays (always with my mother's specialty, chocolate angel-food cake), and birthday parties.

A cat lover from my earliest memories, I noted in my diary the birth of kittens—when their eyes opened, when they first mewed or growled, when my gruff father showed the faintest hint of liking them, and so on. Over the next four years I continued off and on to write my not-very-informative entries. By sixth grade, that small red book reflected a brief spurt of interest in boys, along with a few references to current world events. Several sentences were also written by one or the other of my parents: the dates when my two younger sisters and I had measles and tonsillectomies and the dates when our two remaining grandparents died.

With only ten lines allotted for each day, there was no intrinsic encouragement to wordiness. I now have to deduce the year mostly by my improved penmanship, although I did occasionally write it down as well.

Though verbal and cocky, I was already a stolid child emotionally, carefully hiding my feelings—a characteristic perhaps rooted in my incurring my father's wrath if I ever dared to talk back to him. The description by Swiss therapist Alice Miller of the autocratic life in many families of European background rings a lot of bells for me.[3] My mother and sisters were appalled at the way my father treated me, and all three of them melted into the background during his rages. (I find no hint of those troubled times in my diary.) In retrospect, however, I try to acquiesce in the thought that ". . . the vast majority of human beings are raised by parents who are simply doing the best they can, and who were themselves raised by parents who did the best they could, and so back through the generations."[4]

As a teenager, I either bought or was given an even smaller diary, made of brown leather, with a lock and key. In spite of that token security, however, I never considered writing anything really personal. What if my sisters got into my diary and read it? What if they made fun of me? As a result, many events of those years are lost, and although some are still vivid in my mind, I regret not having my childhood outlook documented in my own words.

I was not at all like Anne Frank, who from her earliest entries viewed her diary, a gift for her thirteenth birthday, as taking the place of the close friend she longed for—one in whom she could safely confide. When my sisters and I eventually cleaned out our parents' house, my mother and father's home for over forty years, we found my shiny red diary but not the brown leather one.

I did not take senior English in high school (I took advanced algebra as an elective instead), but I saw that the teacher of that English class required everyone to make a journal. Each student had a three-ring cardboard folder, for which they chose a title, designed a cover, and then collected things of interest to put in it. Everyone's journal was put on public display, hung on a wire stretched around the classroom. The idea of having a journal enchanted me, and I made such a booklet for myself on my own at home. I called it "On a Tangent," a reflection of my interest in math—and, I now realize, a rather appropriate title metaphorically.

I had begun writing poetry as a ninth grader, when I coedited the junior high newspaper, and I kept all my poems as well as other writing (themes and several autobiographies) in my journal. At age nineteen I became a Christian in college, and I continued writing poetry. I also started two other journals, like the one from high school, with themes and essays from college classes, along with idealistic sayings and passages I had collected from my reading. Those pages were an important part of my adolescent development, and they reflect the person I was becoming and have become.

In other small loose-leaf notebooks I began keeping what might be called "spiritual journals": thoughts, ideas, points made by InterVarsity conference speakers that impressed me, and insights from my own Bible study. Reading those pages now, I am amazed at how abstracted they were from my day-to-day college experience.

Following graduation, I returned to my home state, and after a hard year of attempting to teach and police children at the same time, I got a job teaching English and Spanish at a well-run junior/senior high. In that long-ago and far-away place (Richland Center, Wisconsin) I devised exercises and techniques I now recognize as akin to journal-keeping and unlike anything I had experienced in my own education.

I gave creative writing assignments that focused on what my students "knew firsthand"—how it was for them. To learn grammar, they wrote and diagrammed sentences based on their lives, their friends, school events, and other current happenings. To teach poetry, I gave them a contemporary word or phrase to use as a first-line poetic springboard. The results were surprising, even from students who otherwise got D's in English.

My eighth and ninth graders also wrote detailed and colorful autobiographies. By dividing this autobiographical writing into short segments (which I called chapters), they were able to tell their own stories and have fun doing it.[5] My experience in eliciting that kind of writing from young teenagers encouraged me years later to devise somewhat similar approaches in journal-keeping classes for adults. But that jumps ahead of my story.

During the '60s, I did not write very much, other than (in sequential years) almost daily letters to the two men to whom I eventually became engaged. My marriage in 1966 to Walter Hearn brought an end to a strong undercurrent in my earlier writing: my anguish at being single past age thirty, years longer than my younger sisters and most of my friends. I had been totally socialized into the attitudes about girls and women of my generation: If you did not marry by age twenty-five or, at worst, by age twenty-nine, you were a failure. Marriage was the only acceptable female goal. Nothing in my background made me esteem singleness.

As a teenager I had read Osa Johnson's *I Married Adventure*. As a college freshman studying botany, I wondered if I could become (or marry) a botanical explorer in tropical jungles. I had no realistic vision for a career of my own other than teaching, nursing, or possibly being a librarian. In spite of my limited professional aspirations, however, I eventually became an editor and worked for both InterVarsity Christian Fellowship and the Christian Medical Society until my marriage. To have been "led out of" teaching and "led into" what seemed to me more meaningful work was a great encouragement to my faith. Seven years after marrying, I again began editing and writing as a free-lancer from our home in California.

At the beginning of the '70s, as I reflected on the '60s, I was sorry I had stopped writing about my life during that turbulent era of change. On January 1, 1970, I began what I called a "Chronicle of the '70s." In time, however, that ambitious project waned and lapsed, since I felt that what I had to say was so ordinary. But at the beginning of each new year I would resume my Chronicle, newly determined that it was worth it. Gradually I came to realize that, yes, there were "diamonds in the dust."

At a conference in Saratoga Springs, New York, in 1980, I attended two special sessions on journal-keeping. During subsequent years, I attended every journal-keeping workshop I could find. That coincided with the spread of new approaches to journal-writing pioneered by psychotherapist Ira Progoff as a result of his Jungian studies as well as the development in other circles of Gestalt techniques.

My first workshop was a turning point. After only a few hours, I thought, *I want to do this: I can do this.* Within a year I began teaching a weekend journaling class as an adjunct professor at New College Berkeley, developing ideas as I went along—sometimes right on the spot in the heat of the moment. Some of those ideas proved helpful and others didn't; some I refined further and some I dropped.

As you can see, my perception of journal-keeping first took shape on its own, as I dutifully recorded a few present-tense events of my childhood. In the beginning it was a diarist's typical laundry-list of happenings; gradually it became more of a stream-of-consciousness description of my concerns. Next, the ideas of Progoff and other workshop leaders added motivation, variety, and insight.

Today, I don't write every day, but I do write in phases. My journals reflect how I see myself—as a person, as a Christian, in relation to others and to God. They reveal my questions, as my husband and I ponder God's will for us. I deliberately try to write in good times as well as bad, so that my journal will not become only a "symbol of darkness," an admonition I first heard from Elizabeth O'Connor and took to heart.

Because as a free-lancer I have to, or choose to, bounce a lot of balls, I tend to remain focused on the here-and-now: what I have to do next. At times when I sit down to write in my journal, "I find it so unnatural to rest and reflect that . . . I am often tempted to bolt out the door to slay the day's dragons."[6] As Geraldine Ferraro commented in her autobiography, If I allowed myself to focus only on the emotional, I would become disabled. Or words to that effect. Although I care very much about the emotional level, a lot of the time I just have to move ahead and get the job done. As a strong "J" on the Myers-Briggs personality test, I need closure and a handle on things. Journal-keeping is an aid to that. I am an inveterate list-maker and that, too, is part of journaling. I also fall right between "Thinking/Feeling" on the Myers-Briggs, and my journals reflect that polarity as well.

Since I am sensitive to transitions, phases (chapters) of life, I frequently write about them. But I regard what I write as thoughts or feelings of the moment and not as an overall picture of who I am now or who I will be forever. Although at times I read aloud from my writing to the participants in my workshops, privacy remains a big issue with me.

I am not sure what I will eventually do with my journals; several older women in my workshops have talked to me about that concern as well. For now, though, it is good for me spiritually to have my multiple notebooks (too many to count) with their record of who I was and am.

An observation made by Flannery O'Connor in one of her letters parallels my own experience in journal-keeping: "The first product of self-knowledge [is] humility."[7] The writing I have done about my own life with its ups and downs, and hearing the writing of women and men in my workshops have made me a better, less judgmental, person.

A few lines from a poem by T. S. Eliot summarize my present feelings pretty well:

Because I do not hope to know again
The infirm glory of the positive hour . . .

Because I know that time is always time
And place is always and only place
And what is actual is actual only for one time
And only for one place
I rejoice that things are as they are . . .
. . . I rejoice, having to construct something
Upon which to rejoice

And pray to God to have mercy upon us
And I pray that I may forget
Those matters that with myself I too much discuss
Too much explain.[8]

An End is a Beginning.

The Progoff Method *Appendix*

Ira Progoff, who formulated the principles of "holistic depth psychology," later created what he called the "Intensive Journal" process as a result of his experience as a psychotherapist. Among his many publications, his book *At a Journal Workshop* (an edited transcript of his oral workshop presentations) is best known as the text for his "Intensive Journal" method.

Progoff's organization, Dialogue House (founded in New York City in 1966), continues to hold hundreds of journal workshops each year throughout the U.S. and Canada and several other countries. Now, almost thirty years later, the Dialogue House workshops are led by facilitators trained by Dr. Progoff to lead the various levels of his "Intensive Journal" seminars. Participants receive a large loose-leaf notebook with multicolored dividers separating its four main sections, which are then categorized into twenty-one further segments for individual journal-keeping.

At the heart of Progoff's method is his distinction between "Log" (factual/data-gathering) writing and "Depth Dimension" (amplifying/feedback) writing in the journal notebook. The "depth" material arises from connections perceived when an individual is able imaginatively to descend into the deep "well" of his or her own life. There, Progoff teaches, it is possible to enter an "underground stream": a near-subliminal (intermediate or "twilight") state of consciousness that will help to unify that person's own experience as well as unite him or her empathetically with the rest of humankind.

Everyone's life, Progoff says, has been going somewhere, however blind one may have been to its direction.[1] "The Journal is a way to follow one's own rhythm, to create one's own personal sabbath, whether you come to a workshop or just do it privately in your own life."[2]

One basic aspect of the Progoffian approach to journal-keeping is the writing of dialogues with other persons as well as with one's body, one's work, events, society, and inner wisdom. Not surprisingly, the personification of the "other" in each of those instances is both challenging and helpful. That writing, along with material in the "log" sections, is then amplified in the other categories of the "Intensive Journal," including work with reverie ("twilight imagery") and dreams.

In his book, Progoff's comments about journal-keeping at times take on a tone that leaves me somewhat uncomfortable. He describes reading aloud in a journaling group as placing one's life on an "unseen altar." He sees the "Intensive Journal" as "the sanctuary to which we go for our most intimate and private, our most profound and universal experiences."[3] For most Christians that overstates the case. But for me, as well as for most participants in my workshops, journal-keeping has proven to be a remarkable aid to spiritual growth.

Although the Dialogue House workshops are expensive, any serious journal-keeper would benefit from taking part in one of more of them. (Of the many journal-keeping workshops I have attended in the past decade, all reflect Progoff's groundbreaking work to some degree.) For information about dates and locations of upcoming "Intensive Journal" workshops, call Dialogue House at 800-221-5844. Address: 80 East 11th St., Suite 305, New York, NY 10003-6008.

Endnotes

Note: Full publication information is given here only for books not listed in the bibliography at the end of this book.

Acknowledgments

1. Carlos Fuentes, *Myself with Others: Selected Essays* (Farrar, Straus & Giroux, 1988), 19.

Introduction

1. Elizabeth O'Connor, "On Keeping a Journal," *Letters to Scattered Pilgrims*, 38–39.

2. Since starting work on this book I have wondered where I first heard this phrase, which is so apt a description of my own journal-keeping. It may have been my recollection of a comment by Virginia Woolf: ". . . I have just reread my years [sic] diary & am much struck by the rapid haphazard gallop at which it swings along, sometimes indeed jerking almost intolerably over the cobbles. . . . The advantage of the method is that it sweeps up accidentally several stray matters which I should exclude if I hesitated, but which are the diamonds of the dustheap" (*The Diary of Virginia Woolf*, Volume One 1915–1919, Anne Olivier Bell, ed., Harcourt Brace Jovanovich, 1977), 233–34. Since then, with the help of Mildred Meythaler and the library reference department of Marquette University, I have learned of a book by Jackie Mallis titled *Diamonds in the Dust: Discover and Develop Your Child's Gifts* (1993/1983). Mallis does not cite any source for her title. In early 1994 I also discovered Joni Eareckson Tada's daily devotional guide, *Diamonds in the Dust* (Zondervan, 1993).

3. Quoted in Margaret Craven, *Again Calls the Owl* (Dell Publishing, G. P. Putnam's Sons, 1981), 120.

Chapter 1: Me? Keep a Journal?

1. Karen Mains, "Keeping a Spiritual Diary" (The Chapel of the Air, n.d.), flyer #7384.

2. Susan A. Word, "Love Letters to Myself," *BBW: Big Beautiful Woman*, April 1988, 34.

3. Hundreds of workshops are offered every year in the U.S., Canada, and a number of foreign countries (Australia, Israel, Germany, Japan, and U.K. in 1993–94) by the "Intensive Journal" Program of Dialogue House, an organization founded by Dr. Ira Progoff. Dialogue House (NYC) has a toll-free number, (800) 221-5844. Other authors who lead journal-keeping workshops can be located through information included in their books or through their publisher; see the bibliography.

Journal workshops are offered under various auspices, and the viewpoint of their leaders varies. The approach taken in a particular workshop may relate to the aims of the sponsoring organization. There will probably be differences between workshops held at institutes of noetic sciences or transpersonal psychology, Christian colleges or seminaries, Catholic retreat centers, family counseling services, community colleges, etc. In my opinion, however, you bring to any workshop "the person you are," and you write out of that context.

4. I got the idea of using a loose-leaf journaling notebook, with ordinary dividers, early in 1982 from a workshop not sponsored by Dialogue House but taught by a leader (now deceased) probably influenced by that approach. Elizabeth O'Connor also recommends a loose-leaf notebook in a chapter on journal-keeping included with other essays pertaining to life in the Church of the Saviour community in Washington, D.C. She says: "First, buy a good loose-leaf journal. An investment in a good journal indicates a seriousness of purpose, and will reinforce your belief that a record of your life is worth cherishing" (*Letters to Scattered Pilgrims*, 34). The Progoff "Intensive Journal" workshops (see note 3 above) provide each participant with a large loose-leaf notebook, along with colored dividers for the various segments (twenty-one in all, if you attend the week-long, three-workshop sequence).

5. See "The Progoff Method" in the appendix.

6. Harry J. Cargas and Roger J. Radley, *Keeping a Spiritual Journal*, 8–9.

7. Margaret Hannay and Shirley Nelson, "The Journal: Tool for Discovery," a workshop presented at the 4th National Conference of the Evangelical Women's Caucus ("Women and the Ministry of Reconciliation"), Saratoga Springs, New York, June 25–28, 1980. I am indebted to Anne Eggebroten, now of Santa Monica, California, who encouraged me to attend that conference and sponsored my travel.

8. Charles E. Hummel, *Tyranny of the Urgent*.

9. G. K. Chesterton, "George MacDonald," in *The Chesterton Review*, Vol. xvii, Nos. 3 & 4 (August 1991/November 1991), 287.

10. May Sarton, *House by the Sea: A Journal* (G. K. Hall, 1978), 107, 27–28. Ira Progoff also uses this metaphor in his 1975 guide to journal-keeping.

11. Adapted from an image by Dora Willson in Mary C. Morrison, *The Journal and the Journey*, 13.

12. Hannay and Nelson.

13. O'Connor, 37–39.

14. On the New College workshop evaluations, many people mention that hearing what others have written for a particular exercise was a highlight of the workshop for them; others comment that they regret not having had the courage to read aloud themselves. A letter from *Leland* said it like this: "I wanted to read my free-flow writing aloud; I had been looking at a picture of a grain field surrounded by hills of trees and a beautiful rainbow in the sky with stratus clouds lingering by. I didn't, though, because I had already read aloud once, and I didn't want to monopolize the response time. I was amazed at people's hesitation, because so many of them seemed very talented. I have never claimed to have writing ability, but I have a desire to share. I think you get more out of the workshop when you read aloud, and I know it is helpful to the listeners."

Chapter 2: *Nothing* Never Happens

1. O'Connor, 46, 49.

2. Tristine Rainer describes this "centering process" as a habit of Anaïs Nin, the twentieth-century's most prolific diarist. "Nin . . .

developed the practice of sitting quietly for a few minutes before beginning to write. She would close her eyes and allow the most important incident or feeling of the day or of the period of time since she last wrote to surface in her mind. That incident or feeling became her first sentence. By using this approach you will at least have recorded what is of greatest significance to you, even if you don't have enough time to write everything that you wish to explore" (*The New Diary*), 37.

3. Thomas Mallon, *A Book of One's Own*, xi–xiii.

4. My descriptions of this exercise and the second and fourth ones in this chapter are derived from similar ones titled "Soul Country" and "Time" that originally appeared among thirty-two pages of writing exercises suggested by George F. Simons in his thoughtful and very early (1978) book on journal-keeping (*Keeping Your Personal Journal*), 106–10.

Chapter 3: To Number My Days

1. May Sarton, *Journal of a Solitude*, 13.

2. Luci Shaw, *Life Path: Personal and Spiritual Growth through Journal Writing*, 40. Tristine Rainer devotes an entire chapter to "Overcoming Writing Blocks" with two subtitles, "The Internal Censor and How to Outwit It" and "The Internal Critic and How to Tame It" (*The New Diary*, 215–24). In her 1979 book, Elizabeth O'Connor also referred to what she calls an "internal censorship bureau."

3. Peter Elbow, *Writing without Teachers*, 6–7.

4. Christina Baldwin, *One to One: Self-Understanding through Journal Writing*, 49.

5. Ibid., 99.

Chapter 4: Looking Backwards

1. In *The New Diary* Tristine Rainer describes her approach to listing major events ("stepping-stones") on 77–79. She adds, "You will often discover elements on a list that you wish to explore more intensively through other diary devices." The second major segment of the Progoff "Intensive Journal" notebook, called the Life/Time Dimension, includes among its twenty-one segments a divider with the title, "Stepping Stones."

2. Rosemary Radford Ruether, *Disputed Questions: On Being a Christian* (Orbis, 1989), 12.

3. Flannery O'Connor, *The Habit of Being: Letters*, posthumous (Farrar, Straus & Giroux, 1979), 373, 367.

4. Morton T. Kelsey, *Adventure Inward: Christian Growth through Personal Journal Writing*, 73.

Chapter 5: Chapter (and Verse)

1. The Progoff "Intensive Journal" method begins its basic workshop with writing in a divider category called "Period Log." Tristine Rainer suggests beginning diary writing with the "Present Moment" or the "Present Period," as well as looking for a relevant simile to describe one's life: e.g., "a narrow covered bridge," "a roller-coaster."

Chapter 6: Silencing Your Editor

1. Elbow, 3, 6.

2. Natalie Goldberg, *Wild Mind: Living the Writer's Life*, 10.

Chapter 7: What I Believe and the Difference It Makes

1. This series has appeared in *The Christian Century* over six decades, beginning in 1939. The 1990–1991 articles are reprinted in James M. Wall and David Heim, eds., *How My Mind Has Changed* (Eerdmans, 1991).

Chapter 8: Writing When the Moment Spurs

1. Jon Hassler, *A Green Journey* and *Dear James* (both Ballantine, 1993).

2. Rainer, 100.

3. Ibid.

4. James Hillman, *Insearch: Psychology and Religion* (Scribner's, 1968), 35.

5. Walden Howard, "Personal Growth through Journaling," *Faith at Work* (November 1978). This magazine ceased publication in 1981.

6. Ibid.

Chapter 9: Journal Conversations

1. Rainer, 22, 102.

Chapter 10: Just As I Am

1. George F. Simons, *Journal for Life: Discovering Faith and Values through Journal Keeping*, Part One: Foundations, 4. I first heard the phrase, "The God of Miriam, Deborah, and Huldah," used by Anne McGrew Bennett in an article with that title published in *Right On* (now *Radix* magazine, Box 4307, Berkeley, CA 94704), September 1975. I have worked as copy editor on the staff of *Right On/Radix*, a too-little-known Christian publication, for eighteen years. Luci Shaw, quoted in this book, is *Radix* poetry editor; Sharon Gallagher, its editor.

2. Rick Ocheltree, *Contemporary Designs for Using Intensive Journals as a Means of Nurture in Adult Christian Education*, 6.

3. Cheryl Kimbel Biehl, *Scriptural Meditation: The Listening Side of Prayer*, 55.

4. Categories similar to this one may be titled "Dialogue with a Wisdom Figure," "Dialogue with Someone Wise," or, in the Progoff method, "Inner Wisdom Dialogue."

5. E. B. [Eleanor Elliott Babington], *Poems by Charlotte Elliott with a Memoir*.

6. Harvey Cox, *Just As I Am*, in Robert A. Raines, ed., "Journeys in Faith" series (Abingdon, 1983), 151–52.

Chapter 11: How It Started for Me

1. Eva Hoffman, *Lost in Translation: A Life in a New Language* (E. P. Dutton, 1989), 242, 74.

2. I have also told my story from other perspectives in my two earlier books, *What They Did Right: Reflections on Parents by Their Children* (Tyndale, 1974) and *Our Struggle to Serve: The Stories of 15 Evangelical Women* (Word, 1979).

3. Alice Miller, *For Your Own Good: Hidden Cruelty in Child-rearing and the Roots of Violence* (Farrar, Straus, Giroux, 1983–1984).

4. Christina Baldwin, *One to One*, 66.

5. Writing this, I am well aware of how different the situation is for teachers in many U.S. schools today. A letter I have just received from a friend who works as an interpreter for Russian emigre students in California said: "We're still having fights—and today a rather glamorously dressed Russian girl was brutally beaten up by six or seven Hispanic girls. The incident still hasn't been investigated very thoroughly, due to the huge number of fights today" (October 1993).

An alarming book by William Kilpatrick also emphasizes the great change since the '60s in America's schools. He describes an eighth-grade teacher who tried to focus on what students valued, i.e., what they liked or loved to do. Their response? "Sex, drugs, drinking, and skipping school." (*Why Johnny Can't Tell Right from Wrong: Moral Illiteracy and the Case for Character Education*, Simon & Schuster, 1992), 81.

6. Jan Johnson, "Journaling: Breathing Space in the Spiritual Journey," *Weavings*, March/April 1993, 35.

7. Flannery O'Connor, 125.

8. T. S. Eliot, "Ash Wednesday, 1930," *The Complete Poems and Plays 1909–1950* (Harcourt Brace Jovanovich, 1971).

Appendix: The Progoff Method

1. Ira Progoff, Dialogue House promotional flyer (August 1990), 6.

2. Tom Ferguson, "A Conversation with Ira Progoff," *Medical Self-Care* (n.d.).

3. Ira Progoff, *At a Journal Workshop*, 111, 297.

Bibliography

Books on Journaling from an Explicitly Christian Perspective

Cheryl Kimbel Biehl, *Scriptural Meditation: The Listening Side of Prayer* (Classic Publications, 1981; available for $6.00, postpaid, from P.O. Box 6128, Laguna Niguel, CA 92677).

Christopher Biffle, *Garden in the Snowy Mountains: An Inner Journey with Christ as Your Guide* (Harper & Row, 1989).

Anne Broyles, *Journaling: A Spirit Journey* (The Upper Room, 1988).

Harry J. Cargas, *Exploring Your Inner Space: A Self-Discovery Journal* (St. Anthony Messenger Press, 1991).

Harry J. Cargas and Roger J. Radley, *Keeping a Spiritual Journal* (Doubleday, 1981).

Lura Jane Geiger, et al., *Astonish Me, Yahweh: A Bible-Workbook Journal* (LuraMedia, 1983).

Morton T. Kelsey, *Adventure Inward: Christian Growth through Personal Journal Writing* (Augsburg Fortress, 1980).

Ronald Klug, *How to Keep a Spiritual Journal* (Augsburg, 1993; Bantam Books, 1989; Thomas Nelson, 1982).

———, *My Prayer Journal* (Concordia, 1983).

Peter Lord, *The 2959 Plan: A Guide to Communion with God* (Baker Book House, 1989).

Mary C. Morrison, *The Journal and the Journey* (Pendle Hill Pamphlet, No. 242, Pendle Hill Publications, 1982).

Rick Ocheltree, *Contemporary Designs for Using Intensive Journals as a Means of Nurture in Adult Christian Education* (Unpublished thesis: San Francisco Theological Seminary, 1976).

Elizabeth O'Connor, *Letters to Scattered Pilgrims* (Harper & Row, 1979).

Maria L. Santa-Maria, *Growth through Meditation and Journal Workshops: A Jungian Perspective on Christian Spirituality* (Paulist, 1983).

Luci Shaw, *Life Path: Personal and Spiritual Growth through Journal Writing* (Multnomah, 1991).

George F. Simons, *Journal for Life: Discovering Faith and Values through Journal-Keeping*, Pt. 1, Foundations; Pt. 2, Experience (ACTA, 1975).

———, *Keeping Your Personal Journal* (Ballantine Epiphany, 1986).

Margaret Smith, *Journal Keeper* (Eerdmans, 1992).

Time with God Personal Journal: A Daily Companion for Your Personal Quiet Time; keyed to *Time with God: The New Testament for Busy People: A One Year Devotional/New Century Version* (Word, 1991).

Robert Wood, *Thirty Days Are Not Enough: More Images for Meditative Journaling* (The Upper Room, 1982).

Books on Journaling from Other Perspectives

Christina Baldwin, *Life's Companion: Journal Writing as a Spiritual Quest* (Bantam New Age, 1991).

———, *One to One: Self-Understanding through Journal Writing* (M. Evans, 1977).

Lucia Capacchione, *The Creative Journal: The Art of Finding Yourself* (Swallow Press Books/Ohio University Press, 1979).

Curtis W. Casewit, *The Diary: A Complete Guide to Journal Writing* (Argus Communications, 1982).

Paul S. D'Encarnacao with Patricia W. D'Encarnacao, *The Joy of Journaling* (Eagle Wing Books, Inc., 1991).

Kay Leigh Hagan, *Internal Affairs: A Journalkeeping Workbook for Self-Intimacy* (Harper & Row, 1990).

———, *Prayers to the Moon: Exercises in Self-Reflection* (HarperCollins, 1991). Not as spacey as it sounds.

Thomas Mallon, *A Book of One's Own: People and Their Diaries* (Ticknor & Fields, 1984).

Ira Progoff, *At a Journal Workshop: The Basic Text and Guide for Using the Intensive Journal Process* (Dialogue House, 1975).

———, *At a Journal Workshop: Writing to Access the Power of the Unconscious and Evoke Creative Ability* (J. P. Tarcher, 1992).

Tristine Rainer, *The New Diary: How to Use a Journal for Self-Guidance and Expanded Creativity* (J. P. Tarcher, 1978).

Books on Related Topics

E. B. [Eleanor Elliott Babington], *Poems by Charlotte Elliott with a Memoir* (The Religious Tract Society, 1873).

Marjory Zoet Bankson, *Braided Streams: Esther and a Woman's Way of Growing* (LuraMedia, 1985).

Charles Ben Bissell, *Letters I Never Wrote, Conversations I Never Had* (Macmillan, Collier Books, 1987).

William Bridges, *Transitions: Making Sense of Life's Changes* (Addison-Wesley, 1980).

Frederick Buechner, *Now & Then: A Memoir of Vocation* (HarperCollins, 1983, 1991).

Peter Elbow, *Writing without Teachers* (Oxford University Press, 1973).

Joanna Field (pseudonym for Marion Milner), *A Life of One's Own* (J. P. Tarcher, 1981).

Kathleen R. Fischer, *The Inner Rainbow: The Imagination in Christian Life* (Paulist, 1983).

Carolyn Foster, *Family Patterns Workbook: Breaking Free from Your Past and Creating a Life of Your Own* (J. P. Tarcher, 1993).

Natalie Goldberg, *The Long Quiet Highway: Waking Up in America* (Bantam, 1993).

———, *Wild Mind: Living the Writer's Life* (Bantam, 1990).

———, *Writing Down the Bones: Freeing the Writer Within* (Shambhala, 1986).

B. J. Hateley, *Telling Your Story, Exploring Your Faith: Writing Your Life Story for Personal Insight and Spiritual Growth* (CBP Press, 1985).

Etty Hillesum, *An Interrupted Life: The Diaries of Etty Hillesum 1941–43* (Washington Square Press/Pocket Books, 1981).

Elaine Farris Hughes, *Writing from the Inner Self* (Harper Perennial, 1992).

Charles E. Hummel, *Tyranny of the Urgent* (InterVarsity, 1967), booklet.

John Julian, ed., *A Dictionary of Hymnology* (Dover Publications, 1957).

Morton T. Kelsey, *Dreams: A Way to Listen to God* (Paulist, 1978).

———, *The Other Side of Silence: A Guide to Christian Meditation* (Paulist Press, 1976).

Kenneth Koch, *I Never Told Anybody: Teaching Poetry Writing in a Nursing Home* (Random House, Vintage Books, 1978).

Kathryn Lindskoog, *The Gift of Dreams: A Christian View* (Harper & Row, 1979).

Roseann Lloyd and Richard Solly, *Journey Notes: Writing for Recovery & Spiritual Growth* (Harper/Hazelden, 1989).

Frank Minirth, et al., *Love Hunger Weight-Loss Workbook: A 12 Week Life Plan for the Body, Mind, and Soul* (Thomas Nelson, 1991).

M. Scott Peck, *The Road Less Traveled: A New Psychology of Love, Traditional Values and Spiritual Growth* (Simon & Schuster, 1978).

Ira Progoff, *Depth Psychology & Modern Man* (McGraw-Hill, 1959).

Michael Rubin, *Men without Masks: Writings from the Journals of Modern Men* (Addison-Wesley, 1980).

May Sarton, *Journal of a Solitude* (Norton, 1977); also, other journals by Sarton.

Florida Scott-Maxwell, *The Measure of My Days* (Viking Penguin, 1979).

Susan Shaughnessy, *Walking on Alligators: A Book of Meditations for Writers* (HarperCollins, 1993). Practical, secular.

Ruth Carter Stapleton, *The Gift of Inner Healing* (Word, 1976).

Peter R. Stillman, *Families Writing* (Writer's Digest Books, 1989).

Paula Farrell Sullivan, *The Mystery of My Story: Autobiographical Writing for Personal and Spiritual Development* (Paulist, 1991).

Ronald W. Thomson, *Who's Who of Hymn Writers* (Epworth Press, 1967).

Anne Valley-Fox and Sam Keen, *Your Mythic Journey* (J. P. Tarcher, 1989). Note: This book's earlier title was *Telling Your Story* (Signet, New American Library, 1973).

Dan Wakefield, *The Story of Your Life: Writing a Spiritual Autobiography* (Beacon, 1990).

Katie Funk Wiebe, *Good Times with Old Times: How to Write Your Memoirs* (Herald, 1979).

Magazine and Newspaper Articles on Journal-Keeping

1. The Progoff Method (see the appendix)

R. A. Blake, "Dialogue Weekend: Intensive Journal Workshop" (*America*, February 5, 1977).

Nina Burleigh, "Words of Wisdom: Journaling Gives Voice to the Inner Authority" (*Chicago Tribune*, July 17, 1988).

Tom Ferguson, "A Conversation with Ira Progoff" (*Medical Self-Care*, 1978).

Joseph H. Fichter, "Retreat Method Seeks Inner Tranquility . . . Spiritual Depths 'Beyond Doctrine'" (*National Catholic Reporter*, September 10, 1982); "Repartee" (Letters) in response to Fr. Fichter (*National Catholic Reporter*, October 29, 1982).

Jack Fincher, "Dialogue in a Journal" and "Ira Progoff: Interview" (*Human Behavior: The Newsmagazine of the Social Sciences*, November 1975).

Alicia Fortinberry, "Keeping a Journal for Self-Discovery" and "How to Develop Your Journal" (*New Woman*, January, 1987).

Betty Hansen, "How to Have a Daily Dialogue with Yourself" and "Inmates View Selves through Journals" (*The Saginaw News*, December 3, 1980).

Donna Hardy, "Counselor's Corner" (*Angela Press*, December, 1983).

Bohdan Hodiak, "Journal: Self-Help Way of Riding Out Problems of Change" (*Pittsburgh Post-Gazette*, May 27, 1978).

Rachel Hosmer, The Rev., O.S.H., Review: "The Practice of Process Meditation: The Intensive Journal Way to Spiritual Experience" (*St. Luke's Journal of Theology*, September 1982).

Walden Howard, "Personal Growth through Journaling" (*Faith at Work*, 1978).

"An Introductory Exercise: Working in the Period Log" (*Medical Self-Care*, 1978?).

Robert Blair Kaiser, "The Way of the Journal" (*Psychology Today*, March 1981).

Karolyn Kempner, "Dialog House: Writing Your Way to Wholeness" (*Whole Life Times*, September/October 1981).

"More Than a Hundred Pens . . ." (*Wholeperson Communications*, Vol. IV, No. 2, Early Summer 1984).

Joan Pitlyk, C.S.J., Review: "The Practice of Process Meditation: The Intensive Journal Way to Spiritual Experience" (*Review for Religious*, January-February 1982).

Dannye Romine, "Journal Draws Your Life into Focus" (*The Charlotte Observer*, March 13, 1977).

Ira Progoff, "Simple System to Help You Operate at Your Highest Level" (Dialogue House promotional flyer: "Bottom Line Personal," August 1990).

Beverly Russell, "Dear Diary: A Psychologist's Way to Self-Discovery" (*House & Garden*, June 1976).

———, "The Diary Route to Self-Discovery" (*Decorating: A House & Garden Guide*, Spring 1977).

Harry Scholefield, Review: "At a Journal Workshop" (*Journal of Religion and Health*, Vol. 15, No. 2, 1976).

Kate Scholl, "Our Life's Story as Gift—Why Not Unwrap It This Year?" (*The Candle*, January, 1984).

Edythe Westenhaver, "'Intensive Journal' Wins Creator Worldwide Acclaim among Religious Questers" (Religious News Service, October 23, 1981).

2. Other Approaches to Journal-Keeping

Note: I have not included in this list the many articles that discuss diaries or journals about a single topic (bicycling, camping, children, depression, diets, dreams, fitness and running, family business, fiction-writing, money, nature and the out-of-doors, prison life, teenage writing, tennis, trips and travel, and so on).

Carol Amen, "The Story of Your Life" (*Today's Christian Woman*, Fall 1982).

H. Blodgett, "Dear Diary: How Do I Need You? Let Me Count the Ways" *(The New York Times Book Review*, September 22, 1991).

Conti, "What Do You Write in Your Journal?" *(San Francisco Examiner*, August 19, 1990).

A. Cunningham, "Private Papers" (*Mademoiselle*, July 1991).

G. Daly, "Interview with Thomas Mallon" (*People Weekly*, May 20, 1985).

L. C. DeVona, "Keeping a Daily Journal" (*Blair Ketchums Country*, November 1985).

"A Diary Helps You Discover Yourself" and "Diary May Help in Coping with Stress" (*Monterey Peninsula Herald*, January 15, 1986, and January 26, 1986).

Donna Donahey, "Dialog with Death" (*Journal of Christian Nursing*, Winter 1985).

J. Epstein, "A Mere Journalist" (*American Scholar*, Winter 1985–1986).

E. F. Hailey, "Telling Details" (*Harpers Bazaar*, June 1986).

Donna Jackson, "An Appointment with Myself" (*New Woman*, April 1986).

Jan Johnson, "Journaling: Breathing Space in the Spiritual Journey" (*Weavings*, March/April 1993).

Karen Mains, "Keeping a Spiritual Diary," #7384 (The Chapel of the Air, n.d.).

——, "Shortcuts to a Prayer Journal That Works" (*Christian Herald*, July/August 1986).

J. Moore, "Save Your Life: Notes on the Value of Keeping a Diary" (*Utne Reader*, May/June 1989).

Judith Moore, "Composing the Self" (*The Berkeley Monthly*, June, 1989).

N. O'Neill, "My Mother's Book of Days" (*New Choices for the Best Years*, August 1990).

Bea Pixa, "Keeping a Journal to Learn about Yourself" (*San Francisco Examiner*, October 27, 1980).

Rolland R. Reece, "Discover Yourself" (*Virtue*, January/February 1987).

Sharon Sexton, "Jotting in Your Journal: Diaries Open New Pages to Ourselves" (*USA Today*, April 28, 1983).

Luci Shaw, "Keeping Track of Your Life" (*Today's Christian Woman*, January/February 1988).

Susan A. Word, "Love Letters to Myself" (*BBW: Big Beautiful Woman*, April 1988).

To contact Virginia Hearn about leading a journal-keeping workshop at your church or in your area, write to her in care of the publisher.